THE GOOD THE BAD AND THE DIVORCE

Navigate Your Divorce And Thrive

OSCAR CHAVARRIA

Copyright © 2022 Oscar Chavarria

The Good The Bad and The Divorce
Published in USA and Canada
For additional information about the author visit www.lifebridgecoach.ca
ISBN 978-1-7781596-0-2 (paperback); 978-1-7781596-1-9 (e-Book)

Legal Disclaimer

All rights are reserved. No part of this book may be reproduced or transmitted in any form or by any means, electronic or mechanical, including photocopy, without permission in writing from the author. The author strongly recommends you consult your lawyer before commencing divorce proceedings. The author is not a lawyer and has no expertise in legal advice.

The author provides this book and its contents on an "as is" basis and makes no representations or warranties of any kind with respect to this book or its contents. The author disclaims all such representations and warranties, including but not limited to warranties of legal advice. In addition, the author assumes no responsibility for errors, inaccuracies, omissions, or any other inconsistencies herein.

The author makes no guarantees concerning the level of success you may experience by following the advice and strategies contained in this book, and you accept the risk that results will differ for each individual. Some examples provided in this book may not apply to the average reader and are not intended to represent or guarantee you will achieve the same or similar results.

This book is the result of the author's experience, study and research. The author has made every attempt not to target any living or dead personality/legend, particular person or group of persons or religion or religious place. The names, characters, business, events and incidents are the products of the author's imagination. Any resemblance to actual persons, living or dead, or actual events is purely coincidental and not intended to defame, ridicule, intimidate, annoy or insult anyone, both individually or collectively. The likeness of historical/famous figures has been used fictitiously; the author does not speak for or represent these people. The author in no way represents the companies, corporations, or brands mentioned in this book. All opinions expressed in this book are the author's or fictional.

The content of this book is for informational purposes only and is not intended as legal advice. You understand that this book is not intended as a substitute for consultation with a lawyer. Please consult your lawyer regarding the suggestions and recommendations made in this book.

The use of this book implies your acceptance of this disclaimer. The author shall not be liable for any damages.

CONTENTS

Introduction v

SECTION 1: THE BEGINNING OF A JOURNEY

Chapter 1: Turning a Leaf 3
    Receiving Advice 4
    Perspective 8
Chapter 2: Resolve to Pay the Price Early 15
    Your Lawyer 18
    Next Step, Lawyer Up 23
Chapter 3: Preparing Yourself 35
    Divorce Goals 38
    Dealing with Fear 41
    Higher Thinking 43

SECTION 2: THE PROCESS

Chapter 4: Roadmap 49
    Negotiation 49
    Mediation 50
    Collaborative Divorce 50
    Mediation Plus Each Has a Lawyer 50
    Mediation - Arbitration 62
    Summary Trial 63
    Seven- to Ten-day Full Trial (I hope you don't get to this) 66
    Piecemeal Court Applications 67
    Your Most Likely Path 68
    Walking Toward Peace 68

SECTION 3: TECHNICAL ELEMENTS

Chapter 5: Case Description 73
    JCC - Judicial Case Conference 73

    Retainers 74
    DivorceMate Calculations 75
    Separation Date 76
    Documentation 79
    Views of the Child Report or Section 211 83
    Counselling 86
    False Criminal Charges 87
    Parental Alienation 89
    Children 89
Chapter 6: Technicalities 92
    Representation 92
    Lawyer Quitting 93
    Financing and Contingency 94
    Scheduling Chambers 95
    From the Archives of Experience 97
    Making Mistakes 99

SECTION 4: PSYCHOLOGICAL AND SPIRITUAL DIMENSIONS

Chapter 7: Personality Disorder 105
Chapter 8: Fifty/Fifty Parenting 111
Chapter 9: Finding an Entirely New Meaning 114
Chapter 10: Otherworldly Justice 122
Chapter 11: Remake Yourself 126
    Diet 128
The Next Relationship 131
Closing Thoughts—The Smiling Warrior 135
About The Author 137
Bibliography 139

INTRODUCTION

Buried within the pages of this book, you may just find the golden nuggets that will save you several thousands of dollars in your divorce. As an added bonus, you may find ways to thrive.

I would like to start by saying if there is any chance, even a sliver of hope of saving your marriage, I strongly encourage you to do so. Even the friendliest of divorces is difficult and has the potential of becoming unpredictable.

This book is meant for those who, after much thought, consideration, and sleepless nights, have decided to call it quits.

The specter of divorce never appears suddenly out of the blue in one day. Instead, it appears after months and years of manipulation, verbal/emotional or physical abuse, or constant invasion of personal boundaries. Your reason to seek a divorce may be as simple as the fact that you no longer have anything in common with your spouse, and life has become a bore, a chore, and you know in your bones it is time to move on. More often than not, you stick around because a particular word, "obligation," nags at you. You feel obligated to stick around for the sake of your ex and children. Somehow you have convinced yourself they cannot exist without you, and it is on your shoulders for them to exist. Many times, you stay because you are manipulated into staying by friends and family who convince you that you must stay in a marriage even if you are not happy.

Reasons for staying in a bad marriage are too many to count, but the purpose of this book is not to review all the reasons, rather to help you mitigate and minimize mistakes that I and countless other divorcees have committed.

This book is about going through divorce properly, or at the very least, as properly as it can be done, I do not offer any dirty tricks to help you get an advantage over your ex. In fact, I strongly advise against any dirty tricks.

Statistics clearly indicate that 50% of marriages end up in divorce, and it feels like of the 50% remaining marriages, a good 50% don't really have much of a marriage…their relationship has deteriorated over the years, and they stick together because they are used to it or know no better.

This book is for those who have come to realize the entire purpose of living alongside another human is to be happier than alone. Now you realize that living alone will be infinitely better than to be with the one you married. After tossing and turning at night, trying to figure out your next step, the D word becomes your goal in life. At least in the short term, Divorce is that next step.

My personal journey is not unlike many who have already been there, and I attempt to cover as much of the journey as possible to describe the various paths a process like this may take. Divorce can be an incredibly unpredictable thing, and it is very stressful not knowing what to expect. I hope you will find relief in these pages knowing you are not alone and that there are resources to help you navigate the complex maze of the family law system.

If you do decide to continue reading this book, then let me say this. Divorce is not just an ending, it is a journey of self-discovery, a great opportunity to grow, and yes, there is a light at the end of the tunnel as you are about to embark on a whole new life—after all, I wrote this book, and became a divorce coach.

Through these pages, I intend to help you along your journey and assist you in avoiding the terrible mistakes I, and many others, have made during our respective divorces.

I encourage you to embrace your new journey. You are definitely not alone, many have gone before us, and many will follow. Twenty twenty-one has been known as the year of the great resignation. They seem to be ignoring the fact that 2021 has also been the year of the great divorce, with 2022 following the same trend.

My qualifications—it took me five years of litigation to complete my divorce, and I self-represented in my two-day summary trial. I lost an enormous amount of money in the process. I should be clear though...the money did not go to waste, the lawyers kept it.

I do still thank my lucky star my case did not drag on for countless more years, as some cases have. I visited with twelve lawyers during my journey. As I share this story, combined with the story of many friends, I have replaced their real names with fictitious ones.

The various stages of divorce as described in this book will apply to most people. However, legal processes may differ in your province or state.

While I lightly touch on various challenges of the human condition, this book does not deal with the intricacies of navigating the maze of substance abuse, mental illness, physical abuse, violence, and the myriad of pathological and psychological conditions existing today. Issues like these can create extreme hardships in the best of marriages.

Let me say congratulations for picking up this book and having a genuine interest to improve your situation.

Note: All citations are indicated with a number in brackets i.e. [1], and a referenced bibliography is located on the last page.

SECTION I

The Beginning of a Journey

CHAPTER 1

Turning a Leaf

Memories of the good old days are fresh in your mind. You can still remember when you would fall asleep as soon as your head hit the pillow, when you enjoyed finishing work to go back home to do fun things with your spouse—sports, dining, home projects, and you name it.

Lately you spend more time at work, sleep doesn't come easy, and you prefer to do things on your own. Some time ago, marriage felt as if two rivers converged into one big stream, and energy flowed into it. Now it feels more like the same stream is about to run into a waterfall. There is a feeling like undigested food. You know it bothers you but prefer not to think about it in hopes it will go away by itself, but it does not. Things have changed, and you know you are about to turn a leaf in life.

I've written the following pages specifically for those individuals who have completely resolved that divorce is the next step in life. I do, however, still cover the "thinking about it" phase, that period of uncertainty when your vision is blurred…you are not sure if the river stream is headed to a waterfall or simply running through turbulence caused by rocks in the riverbed, and it is difficult to ascertain which one it is.

As you've likely guessed, it's best to avoid divorce litigation if there's any chance of it. I compare divorce litigation to this type of scenario: You are in jail and ready to leave but the guards tell you that you must solve a Rubik's cube in ten minutes before you are let outside. The problem is you have never touched one of these cubes before. Not an ideal situation, is it?

In divorce, nobody provides clarity on how to navigate. The only suggestion you can get from friends and family is "speak to a lawyer," but they don't tell you HOW to speak to one and how to navigate the maze you are about to enter. In my case, I felt like I fell short solving the "Rubik's cube" scenario...I was on my own.

Receiving Advice

When you're still in the "thinking about it stage," you are in the ambivalent zone, and it is hard to decide your next step in life. Should you stay in this unhappy marriage or divorce? The more you think about it, the more you realize you should end your marriage and start the divorce process. You may need to speak with your friends and brainstorm ideas, gaining confirmation of your thoughts. You know what you are thinking but you still need another person to validate your own mental process during this stressful time.

As it turns out, no matter how much you care about them and they care about you, most of the time friends and family are the worst individuals to approach for advice. Following are just a few of the reasons:

> A. Family may be too emotionally invested and tell you to "Get an aggressive lawyer." Friends may be so disconnected from your situation they may likely say, "Fix your marriage." It seems these two answers are the most commonly agreed upon, socially acceptable answers today. However, either answer

requires an enormous amount of work and effort, but more importantly, which advice is right and how do you decide? Family may get so involved that you find yourself investing an enormous amount of time and energy explaining yourself and having to deal with their frustrations, and friends can simply be too detached from the situation to give proper advice.

B. If you happen to be divorcing a spouse with a personality disorder, understand this very early in the process: hardly anyone will be able to understand what you are going through. If you are in this situation, I strongly recommend searching for Doctor Ramani on YouTube. She provides great information on personality disorders.

C. If your family and friends agree with you that divorce is the right thing for you, oftentimes they will proceed with legal advice, which likely will be wrong. The only way they can give you correct advice is if they themselves have gone through a high conflict, litigious divorce. If they do not have this kind of experience, often, their advice will be mostly useless.

A friend of mine kept referring to her divorce as extremely difficult and high conflict. A couple of weeks into our conversation I asked her how much she spent on litigation and how long it took her, expecting to hear many years and several thousands. She responded she spent $500 certifying the agreement both had signed, and it took her a couple of nights to make her ex understand the agreement was the only way to go. For her, this was a high-conflict divorce! She never knew she had one of the friendliest of divorces.

The reality is that in the minds and hearts of most divorcees, any divorce is extraordinarily difficult and high conflict, no matter how friendly it actually was. What kind of advice would my friend give to someone who is heading to the courts?

You can see how her perspective would not lend itself to provide you with advice in a more contentious situation, and how this is shaping up to be a lonesome journey for you. In reality you don't have many people to talk to and guide you...actually, very likely you don't have anyone to have a meaningful conversation with that includes strategy and real-world instructions on what to do next. Then there are those who may advise you to "destroy your ex and take them to the cleaners." This particular advice seems to be quite popular and is responsible for many ills in society today.

The divorce process is not about winning and destroying the other—it is about continuing your divorce journey with the least number of mistakes, in the shortest possible time frame and the most amicable way available. The point is, whichever direction your divorce will take, you will want to know as early as possible and prepare accordingly.

If you happen to be in the ambivalent zone of still thinking about divorce, but you can't find someone to talk to, one way to begin your journey is by journaling. It is an extraordinary tool; I began journaling when in this zone and found that once I reflected on my own printed words, I understood what my next step should be. Writing your thoughts down is a powerful way to bring clarity into your world. In a way, you become your very own coach/counsel, and begin to trust your intuition. If there is ever a situation when a human must make good use of their intuition, this is it.

Reading books on law and personal improvement are great help as well. You are about to embark on a do-it-yourself for yourself project, and you owe it to yourself to be as ready as possible. While it may not be easy to find the proper support group, your mind and intuition will guide you all the way to the finish line. One of the reasons divorce is such an opportunity to grow is that it stretches your abilities to the limit, and makes you try disciplines you had never considered before.

In the very beginning I did not journal, read books, or plan, so my first divorce attempt failed. This idea of attempting to divorce and then reconcile seldom works. It is not a stretch to say that this "reconciliation" may feel more like a pretense. Scenarios like this repeat themselves frequently in many marriages. Isolation and lack of proper psychological support during this time will make one's thinking clouded and inhibit the ability to make proper decisions.

The big **D** (divorce) should never be used as an instrument of discipline to square and bring your spouse into line, and glue the marriage back together. These tactics are quite damaging, and if it is happening in your life, it may just be a pretty strong indication that divorce is indeed the way forward. The word divorce should never be used lightly in a marriage. Once used, it will be acted upon sooner or later. It really does not help your situation to start the process, only to abort later. It will leave scars that rarely ever heal and brings a new dynamic of distrust and secrecy into an already bad marriage.

However, if you are in a place where there is a possibility of fixing your marriage, then you should do so. The big **D** should only be used once all remedies have been tried and efforts exhausted.

It can only help your case to have a road map clearly traced in your mind, or better yet, have your thoughts in writing (as if it were a business plan), before declaring your desire to divorce. It is far easier to stick to a plan as you go through the motions than to make things up as you go along, which is what most of us do with disastrous results.

Perspective

Once you have tried everything to sort out your divorce in the most amicable way possible, for a number of weeks, months, or even years, you may find yourself in that place with the unavoidable conclusion that legal action is the only way to move forward. Naturally, you dread the idea because no matter how little or how much you know about family law, you know one thing for certain—legal fees are expensive. Currently legal fees are $250 to $450/hour (or more), so you are right in wanting to avoid the financial fallout of starting legal action. But, what do you do if there is no other alternative and your ex refuses to negotiate?

Let's take a moment to understand where you are at, taking up the decision to commence legal action. Before arriving at this point you have been unhappy in your marriage for a while, months or even years. Maybe you have already tried to end the relationship in an amicable manner to no avail. You are angry at the way things have evolved, or perhaps we should say "devolved." Your thinking is clouded, you are worried and anxious, depressed, and tense. You have reached the end of the relationship and are about to call it quits. About this time you want to settle your affairs tomorrow and be on your way.

I refer to this as the "disconnected zone." Emotionally and mentally, you are already many miles away from the marriage and the family home, but in the eyes of the law you are still as happily married as when you said, "I do."

Can you see the disconnect already? Emotionally and mentally, you have already crossed the finish line, but from the legal perspective you have not even made reservations for your journey.

Succinctly put, you are about to start a legal journey which requires calm, reflection, rational thought, analysis, intelligence, patience, and restraint, at a time when you are ready to bolt. What's worse, you don't really have someone to talk to. Most people in your circle can't really give you meaningful advice. I discovered that those who have never been divorced love to give advice about something they know nothing about and claim to know the law quite well.

For example, some friends and family may be quick to exclaim, "Lawyer Up!" and encourage you to get an aggressive lawyer after you inform them of your impending divorce. They may speak with full conviction as if they have been through divorce numerous times and know more about the legal system than anyone around. Again, they fail to mention **HOW** to go about it.

Let's put this "Lawyer Up!" into perspective. The following analogy may help with understanding the advice others may give you within the context of the journey you are about to embark on.

Suppose you tell your non-athletic best friend, who has never hiked in his life that you plan to climb Mount Kilimanjaro. He immediately responds, "Make sure you take nice T-shirts."

You don't know anything about climbing, so taking his advice, you buy some charming T-shirts, flight, and train tickets to Mount Kilimanjaro. Armed with nice tees, you are sure to reach the peak. After all, you trust your friend—what could possibly go wrong?

Once you get there, everyone notices you have some cash to spend. Nobody tells you how badly prepared you are, and tees are useless on your journey. Instead, they sell you all kinds of souvenirs, making you think that is what you need in order to climb. Nobody stops to mention you need a minimum of two years training.

You start the adventure, and about two hundred feet into your four-mile journey, you are tired, out of breath, and out several thousand of dollars already. You retreat to base camp and go home.

On your way home, you begin to recollect all that bad advice you were given, and you still cannot quite figure out what exactly went wrong. Your friends would never mislead you. What just happened?

As you will see in the following pages, the "Lawyer Up!" advice you received from friends and family is just as useful as being told to get a nice tee. I had absolutely no idea what I was in for at the start of my journey, but I kept my nice tees.

Lots of work, time, money, and effort goes into finding, retaining, and working with a lawyer until the end of your case. Nobody around tells you about the intricacies of finding and dealing with one, which in itself seems to require an extensive set of skills that most of us simply don't have. Good advice, at a time when you need it most, is really hard to come by.

My divorce took five years. I met with twelve lawyers and retained seven. As you might expect, it was costly and high conflict.

I can confidently say that I have much to share with you in the hopes of making your own climb easier, and help you become better prepared mentally and emotionally for your upcoming journey. Half the battle is understanding what you are about to walk into. The family law machine is nothing short of entering the Twilight Zone, where up means down, left means right, and straight is backwards. Nothing about it makes sense. When you step back and look from a distance you can appreciate that there really is no reason why a divorce should cost several tens or hundreds of thousands of dollars.

When my journey began, I was adamant and even foolishly stubborn to avoid at all costs the prospects of going into trial. I was scared of the word "trial" and was simply not ready to even hear it. Yet, that is exactly what I needed to hear and understand. Had a good lawyer shaken me up and shot painful arrows of truth straight into my thick skull, they would have told me there was no way to avoid it and that I should have been ready for a trial from the get-go. Why didn't I hear this advice before almost two years into my process?

My own reluctance to accept the prospect of trial early in the process came back to bite me in more ways than once.

I believe that a lawyer with a few years of experience should be able to tell, within the first few days of handling your case, where your divorce is headed and have a strong opinion as to which of the available resolution paths your case will take:

- ✓ Negotiation
- ✓ Mediation
- ✓ Collaborative Divorce
- ✓ Piecemeal Court Applications
- ✓ Arbitration
- ✓ Summary Trial
- ✓ Seven- to Ten-day Trial

Very often they, however, do not tell you this. Lawyers will keep telling you things like, "And now let's try this, and now let's try that. Let's try to negotiate, let's try to mediate and see what kind of results we can get."

Your job is to be at the wheel of your case and learn how to ask questions. I would go as far as saying it is your duty to ask questions. Divorce is not simple math where 10 - 20 = -10. In many ways it is like playing 3D chess where there are a large number of moves and countermoves available at every step. A habit of asking your lawyer pertinent and smart questions will also help trigger new ideas and see if there are better alternatives. Remember, lawyers are human, and you need to work with and nudge them with smart, pertinent questions along the way.

Have you played Solitaire and, at some point, found that you have been missing some pretty obvious moves for a long time? It's irritating, isn't it? Lawyers have knowledge of the system, but they may be missing an obvious move, and they may just think of it when you ask questions. It requires a synergistic lawyer-client relationship where both need to hash things out to determine the next step. I do not recommend just pushing your case over to your lawyer and letting them take care of everything. The more involved you are, the greater the likelihood you will inspire them to be more passionate about your case.

Legal negotiations will commence once a lawyer on either side is retained and sends a letter expressing the spouse's wish to proceed with divorce. The receiving spouse has no other choice but to also get a lawyer to be able to respond.

When you and your spouse both have lawyers, two complete strangers enter into the picture and dig deep— I mean very deep, into all of your finances, earnings, savings, net worth, and personal life, sex life, and all of it. Yes, they investigate your personal life, from breakfast routines and all of it. That private life you never discuss with friends and family, you are about to disclose to two complete strangers who happen to be getting paid hourly to hear it. Indeed, it is difficult to find dignity in this process.

My own journey began very naively. Before I started my divorce legal action, I had read that 95% of court filings settle out of court. I felt the odds were greatly in our favor and we would be able to settle this in a very short time and inexpensively. I simply had no idea I was heading straight into Mount Kilimanjaro. Onward I went with my nice tees.

The process of divorce litigation makes no sense, so even when you try to explain it to intelligent people, they cannot understand what you are saying. You end up even more frustrated because you have to explain yourself to the very friends you are trying to have an intelligent conversation with. Soon you realize it is best to just not say anything.

Simply put, you are ending a broken marriage and about to enter the ~~twilight zone~~ Family Law System, which can be extremely unpredictable. It is a real challenge to enter this zone, even in the best of mental and emotional states—just imagine what it's like when your mind is fogged up.

Graph representing your vision of divorce

Decision to divorce ⎯⎯⎯⎯⎯⎯⎯➤ Divorced!

What divorce may end up looking like

Decision to divorce   [scribbled chaotic line]   ➤ Divorced!

I can say with all certainty now, if I had only known then what I know now, I would have made much better choices. Instead, my divorce experience ended up looking like the second sketch above. It took me five years to get divorced! Yes, I did speak to lawyers, twelve of them. But no one explained the process and the different stages.

Divorce is a risk. Staying in a broken marriage is, too. So by definition there is no way to eliminate risk whatever you do. However, there are steps you can take to mitigate risk, minimize mistakes, and make your divorce process a little smoother with a road map. Nice tees don't help.

Now, it is worth mentioning that the Family Law Act in Canada on its own is very thorough, comprehensive, and extremely fair. It has evolved over many years out of common law, and it is the result of documenting countless divorce trials over many years. Tremendous effort has been put into making this act as fair as it can be. It is my opinion that the act is fair and worth gold.

Unfortunately, a handful of aggressive lawyers can and will mess with due process to prolong the conflict, enriching themselves along the way. It just takes one unethical lawyer in the mix for your divorce to go south. They can be on your side or the opposite side, either way they can inflict great pain if they so choose. Your job is to be honest with yourself, assess the situation early, make smart decisions, and mitigate this risk as much as possible.

CHAPTER 2

Resolve to Pay the Price Early

Stories abound of individuals who refused to put up a legal defense in order to avoid conflict, or their defense was so weak they might as well not have had any at all. It is very common to hear, "I did not want any more conflict and headaches, so I walked away and just let the other side push their paperwork into mediation/court/arbitration." Typically, the person relating a story like this was taken to the cleaners.

At first you may think this reasoning makes sense. After all, avoiding conflict and leaving a relationship in the best possible manner and not creating a ruckus is the high road. Conflict avoidance is what all mature adults want.

In my view, very few other events in life will push you and stretch your mind as much to evaluate morality, religion, ethics, law, philosophy, accounting, and contractual obligations more than a divorce. It really puts you to the test. You may be inclined to say, "I will leave everything to my spouse, avoid conflict, and be on my way." I get it! I know exactly why you would want to do this. However, if this describes you, I highly encourage you to reconsider your position. Here are just a few out of many reasons why you should reconsider:

A. The financial loss can be so tremendous you may end up feeling its impact the rest of your life. Perhaps you are destined to make millions after divorce, in which case whatever you lose in divorce will be a wash. But if you do not become a millionaire, the results of an unfair division of assets can be crippling for many years to come.

B. Judgement by close friends and family when they hear your story and wonder in their minds, "You let your ex take you to the cleaners, just like that?" Even worse, what if they say it to your face...how humiliating!

C. If you happen to be the better parent, your kids will, one day, wonder why you did not fight for them to get equal parenting time. Why would you not fight for a more equitable division of assets so they will have the freedom to choose which parent to spend more time with as they grow older? If the division of assets is such that one parent is taken to the cleaners, then there is a good chance kids will want to spend less time with that parent.

D. Your kids deserve to see each parent on equal financial footing after a divorce.

E. Nobody can possibly know what the "winning" spouse will do with the money if that spouse takes all or nearly all. What if they marry a gold digger, gamble, go on expensive vacations, become a drug/alcohol addict, etc., and end up losing everything later? Then the family will really have lost everything.

F. Do not think for a minute that your ex will either like or respect you any more by letting them have most of your assets, in fact, quite the contrary. They lose even more respect for you—In their minds, if you let yourself be taken, then you also deserve to be kicked, kicked often, and kicked hard. This scenario is even more likely to develop if it is the healthy spouse starting the divorce process.

G. Nobody will thank you for giving up what rightfully belongs to you. I think it is worth repeating—nobody will thank you for giving up what rightfully belongs to you. In fact, it may potentially strain your future relationships.

H. Are you considering giving the farm away as a form of atonement for your perhaps unfounded sense of guilt? Somehow you have convinced yourself that letting your ex keep everything will absolve you of all the wrongs you have committed. It simply does not work that way. Monetary transactions cannot be used in place of what should be soul searching and inner healing.

No matter what you decide to do, you will most definitely pay a price. If you do not pay the price of a proper and fair division of assets now, you may pay for it the rest of your life.

Resolve to pay the price now—not later. The fair price to pay is a fifty/fifty division of assets accumulated during the marriage and equal parenting time, plain and simple. You must not try to take more than your fifty per cent, for doing so will create the karmic conditions in your life that you will have to pay it back with interest. There are those divorce cases with no children in the marriage, and one spouse did either nothing or very little to contribute to the family wealth, and likely should not even get that fifty percent. Probably this is the reason for the divorce, and most likely they will indeed get half of it in court.

Karma is the iron-fisted universal law that no human can escape from, and the future will ensure we all pay our dues.

Karma will most certainly visit the miscreants who take innocent spouses to the cleaners. The same pain they cause will return to them, an absolute universal fact.

Your Lawyer

So what exactly does "Lawyer Up!" really mean? How do you go about it? How do you even begin? I had these and many more questions when I started my high conflict divorce journey. I actually had no idea how to start the process.

I read three books written by experienced lawyers and found them to be full of mostly anecdotes, without much practical information on how to go about your own divorce. I expected these books to provide useful legal information. I noticed they were very careful to not offer much real advice.

Some of these books claimed you could handle your own divorce if only you prepare and organize your material evidence properly. I discovered if you are going to the Supreme Court without either full representation or unbundled legal services, then you have a steep mountain to climb—doable, but extraordinarily hard work required. Supreme Court is a very complicated and highly technical place, and going at it alone is a tall order. It is not enough to have all the documents and evidence required for your case if you don't know how to package it and present it to a judge. A judge will never be impressed by your nice tee.

After going through my own personal journey, talking to fellow divorcees, and reading about other cases, I found the steps toward divorce are the same in over eighty percent of the cases. The remaining percent I do not cover here are cases where there is physical abuse, violence, severe mental disorders, and false criminal accusations. I think even lawyers have a heck of a time with these types of cases.

As I inventoried reasons that prevented me from taking legal action earlier than I did, I realized just how much I feared ending up in a full family trial. I was downright scared of going to court, as I always knew the financial cost would be enormous. I was really afraid of going into financial Armageddon, and at the end we both could end up losing it all in a senseless legal battle. In 2017 you could not find anyone more scared of going to court than me. As a result, I was incredibly unprepared to speak to a lawyer.

Lawyers, like engineers, doctors, architects, etc. are not born, but made after birth…and they want what any other human wants. They want to pay off the student loan, which likely is in the several tens of thousands. They desire to get married, have children, own a home, own two cars, own a vacation cabin, travel the world, and go to fancy restaurants. Yes, lawyers have dreams like any other human, and they will work hard to get to those dreams, just like anyone else.

Many will work overtime, evenings, and weekends to reach their goals. It is a long road ahead and they know it. There is much to accomplish for a single lifetime, and the pressure is on to perform.

We need lawyers as much as we need architects, doctors, and computer programmers. There is just no way around this. Lawyers have spent countless hours studying law and practicing. They have the knowledge and experience we need to go to legal war. Until radical, extreme, and positive changes are implemented in the court system, lawyers will be needed.

Remember, before you start working with a lawyer you are dealing with a human being who has their own dreams, aspirations, and goals. It so happens you will be a paying client who will help them reach those goals. Business 101. Remember, before your lawyer starts working for you, they are working to reach their own goals.

Then you have a few unethical lawyers who will not hesitate to create a huge legal battle for their benefit. All they need to know is the net worth in the family to understand that a litigious divorce is nice to have. A personality-disordered client with a healthy net worth is pure gold for them. The problem is compounded when these lawyers don't really need to understand the law well—they just need to know the tricks of the trade, which can take them far.

In my opinion, these lawyers are in the minority, and the odds are in your favor you will not run into one, but they are most definitely there.

Remember, nobody will have greater interest in your case more than you and you alone.

A divorce process is extremely important and will have a tremendous impact for the rest of your life on you and your children. You cannot afford to simply drop your case on a stranger's desk and hope for the best.

I have met people who did not take their divorce seriously. They did not read any books on the subject, did not prepare, did not visualize a fair outcome, and did not do anything to show they were interested in their own futures. Those individuals settled for tremendously unfair deals and gave the farm to the ex, just because they did not want to deal with the headache or as a form of attornment, only later to regret their mistakes for years to come. The financial impact of your settlement may potentially last for the rest of your life.

Once you settle and sign on the dotted line it's done, no going back.

You need to know what legal options are available to you and which option is the best fit for your case. As we are about to see in next chapters, there are different ways of arriving at a settlement, but you must know what they are and explore them thoroughly. Many times your lawyer will not take the time to properly explain these to you (as it happened to me). I've listed options below. It's your responsibility to understand what they are and then ascertain the best path for your situation:

- ✓ Negotiation
- ✓ Mediation
- ✓ Collaborative Divorce
- ✓ Piecemeal Court Applications
- ✓ Arbitration
- ✓ Summary Trial
- ✓ Seven- to Ten-day Trial

After deciding the best path, you can decide whether you want full representation, unbundled legal assistance, or no legal help. Even with no legal help, there is much you can do to present your case in court. Do not give up. It won't be easy, but it's not impossible, either.

Once you start the divorce process it is important to be firm in your resolve without hesitation. Hesitation in divorce creates added damage for everyone. You want to explore friendly ways to divorce, but you must always move forward to the next step as quick as possible.

After our first separation, we reconciled. I needed more time to gather the resolve to proceed legally. Looking back, I can see that all that hesitation was very damaging for everyone. At that time, I also received terrible advice from friends and even one lawyer, who said, "Fix your marriage."

Alan, one of the lawyers I visited, actually felt terrible for my ex. He succinctly told me I was wrong for thinking about divorce. Of course, I did not retain him, but here is the question that must always remain in your mind: is my lawyer working for me or do they secretly want my ex to win? Here comes one of the great paradoxes of your case— just because you have retained a lawyer does not mean they are genuinely invested in your case.

You must remain vigilant to understand where you really stand. While working with James, Charles, and Bob, I had a sneaky feeling about their true intentions—that they were not on my side a hundred percent. Sometimes a sneaky feeling comes after a few incidents that, while not major on their own, combined give you that unsettling feeling.

When Charles represented me in a chamber's application, he did not know the applicable case law that applied to my case and gave me bad advice. At chambers he was ill prepared, stumbling and fumbling. He could not even remember my name, a disaster. I felt like the outcome of my case was just not important to him. I was just one more chump who walked into his office. He was so oblivious to his own inadequacy that he was convinced I would keep him for the rest of my case.

In my first conversation with another lawyer, Michael, I asked if it was possible for my ex to keep all the assets (I am paraphrasing slightly). He responded that she may. I followed with another question: are rulings like this where one spouse takes everything typical in court? He answered no. I followed up again asking how common is it to divide all assets fairly, and he said fairly common.

Had I not followed up with some very simple and relevant questions to my initial inquiry, Michael would have had me convinced there was no point in going to court and I should just accept my fate. A few additional simple questions allowed me to determine I needed to push forward.

This scenario may appear and repeat in your case, too. You will be told something as if it was a fact of life, but if you follow up with prompt and skillful questions, you will likely find out your options and chances are much better than what you were originally told. There is no way around it. You must do some homework and acquire a basic understanding of your legal rights. It is right and fair for you to assume a trial outcome resulting in a fifty/fifty split and parenting time—it is on you to have a basic understanding of the Family Law Act (or equivalent for your country and state).

Next Step, Lawyer Up

Now that you know and understand your future lawyer is a human with their own dreams, your job is to find one whose dreams and passions line up with yours so you can work together. It is not just about the money. Your ideal human is one who takes pride in the work they do and has a genuine interest in their clients' cases.

How do you find your lawyer? Personal recommendations are always the best start.

If you are unable to find a recommendation, then you must do your homework and hunt for one. I recommend putting lots of effort into this stage, as everything will hinge on your selection. Measure twice, cut once. Measure four times if you have to.

Most lawyers will charge you for an initial meeting. While it is painful to have to pay for an initial meeting, I recommend you meet with at least four lawyers. This will help you get the right one at the onset. If you hire the wrong lawyer, it will cost you later. While it may seem like a waste of money and time to meet with four lawyers at the beginning of your case, it will be money well spent. Deciding on the right lawyer for you at the onset may translate into tens of thousands in savings at the end of your case.

Before you call any lawyers, though, you must do some research on the ones you are considering, and use every available tool to do so. Here are just a few suggestions:

- ✓ Go to Google Maps and type in family law lawyers. Read up on the reviews, the law firms, the lawyers' bios, and carefully comb through their websites.
- ✓ Go to Yelp and read the reviews.
- ✓ Go to LawyerRatings and look up their names: https://www.lawyerratingz.com
- ✓ Go to LinkedIn, Facebook, Twitter, and all social media to see what you can find out about your shortlisted names.

You will want to collect as much information about your potential legal counsel ahead of the first meeting so you'll have a good idea of what to expect.

At one time I was recommended a lawyer, and I visited her website, which was nothing but a picture of her and the placeholder words of the website template. My impression was that if she did not care about her website, then likely she would not care about my case, so I did not call her.

In short, you can do a tremendous amount of qualification before you even pick up the phone, which I highly recommend. Always do your homework ahead of time every step of the way, especially in the beginning. If you get it right, then the rest of your journey will be that much easier (of course "easier" is just a relative term).

Do not be fooled into thinking that high price lawyers are the best option to have just because they are expensive. Actually, I made this foolish mistake when I retained Charles. I did not understand he was spending more time dreaming about the beach than doing a good job. The fact is that young lawyers are full of energy, stamina, and eager to make a name for themselves. So do not discount young lawyers because of their apparent "lack of experience" or the fact that their rates are lower than more experienced lawyers. Many times, these younger men and women are quite capable of providing you with top notch services. Both John and Michael are two young lawyers I retained, and both were extraordinarily smart, talented, and highly ethical.

Now that you have your shortlist of four names, it is time to take the first step toward making an appointment. My first e-mail to the lawyer was extremely short and to the point: are you accepting new clients? There is no point in saying much else if they are busy and cannot take your case.

I sent so many first-contact e-mails that I created a document indicating whom I e-mailed and when. I also wrote their responses in this document, just to keep record of my conversations. When making an appointment, get the hourly rate. It should be a single dollar amount such as $300/hr. and not a range like $300 - $400.

When going to your first appointment, arm yourself with a list of questions. Typically, on the first interview the lawyer will ask you many questions. Make sure you have enough time to answer them and also have time to ask your own questions. The first meeting is meant to understand if you two are a match and can work together, so it must be a two-way conversation where both of you disclose personal/professional information.

Some sample questions you may want to ask include:
- ✓ How long have you been practicing family law?
- ✓ How many divorces have you represented thus far?
- ✓ How many have you solved through direct negotiation with the other party?
- ✓ How many through mediation?

- ✓ How many through mediation arbitration?
- ✓ How many through summary trial?
- ✓ How many through full trial?
- ✓ How many cases are you handling at the moment?
- ✓ How many hours will it take to complete the next actionable item? Typically this includes sending off completed documents or letters.

The above is a good list for starters, and add as you see fit. I cannot overemphasize the need for these questions. Some lawyers specialize in certain areas of resolution more than others. For example, some prefer to resolve a conflict through summary trial, others through full trial.

Yes, being the humans they are, lawyers will naturally find their own niche of conflict resolution and will steer you in a certain way. This is one reason it's important to explore the different types of conflict resolution early in the game, starting from the friendliest form up to the most acrimonious, which is full trial.

When visiting lawyers, make sure to create a contact record for them and make notes about all the relevant points from your conversation. It is very helpful in case you want to refer to those notes in the future. It is a huge help in case you need to drop your first lawyer and hire the second option on your list. You will be able to find all the necessary information in your computer.

Before meeting a lawyer, I always wrote my questions in my computer Notes, and would write down the answers and comments under my questions in the same note. Often times I would migrate my notes over to the contact card as well, so I would have a copy of the conversations I had with every lawyer in an easy-to-find place.

In other words, you need to draw up your very own legal case road map. Preferably put all your thoughts on your laptop. I would never have been able to complete this journey without my beloved laptop, smartphone, cloud storage, and a very healthy cellular data plan.

Introductory meetings with four lawyers may run you around $1,500, which may seem like a ton of money for a bunch of first meetings. But please learn from my mistakes…I know from experience, picking the wrong human to represent your case will be infinitely more expensive than $1,500. This is one little piece of advice I wish someone had told me. I strongly advise you to put in lots of effort, making the time and financial investment to ensure you find the right human at the start of your journey.

The other reason to meet with at least four lawyers from the get-go is that if you need to fire your first pick down the road, you will already have a second choice to go to in short order without losing too much time in transition between lawyers. Again, you will want to complete your process in as short period of time as possible. Dragging things on is tremendously damaging and costly.

The first one-hour meeting should feel like a business meeting and yet be a comfortable personal conversation. You should both feel comfortable asking and responding to questions… the conversation should feel like it has a natural ebb and flow where one person speaks and the other listens without constantly interrupting, and there is a perception the other is listening to the one speaking.

It should feel like meeting someone in a food court at the table next to you and you discover he is a roofer. You tell him you are looking to replace your roof in the summer, and minutes later he gives you a business card. He proceeds to explain about his many years of professional experience. The conversation goes well, it feels good. You check everything you can about his business, and once satisfied you call him to fix your roof. Your conversation with your to-be lawyer should have this type of feeling, too.

It is reasonable for the lawyer to offer you a commentary of what your case looks like from the legal perspective. There must be a feeling that you both connect. Yet, it's all serious business.

Some red flags are:
- ✓ Constant interruption in the middle of someone's sentence.
- ✓ Lawyer asks questions as if they are investigating you, hardly looking up to make eye contact.
- ✓ Keeps their head down, furiously making notes.
- ✓ You come out feeling like you have just been interrogated by the police.
- ✓ Spending too much time talking about topics other than your case, i.e. politics, vacation spots, real estate markets, latest news reports, etc. This is a business meeting, and it must be conducted as such. Some pleasantries are important, but they must be in moderation. After all, you are paying.
- ✓ Their eyes light up when you mention the family's net worth. Keep an eye out for body language.
- ✓ They offer to finance their services. This one is real tricky as there may be cases when it is necessary to make such arrangements. By and large, I advise against it. If possible, it is far better to borrow the money than to get financing from the lawyer. This arrangement may just come with its own can of worms (on top of the divorce you are trying to deal with). Very few lawyers offer this kind of arrangement.

It is not advisable to change horses in the middle of the river, as they would say. But if your horse is sick and cannot make it across, you may very well have to.

When I met with Wilson, I knew he was not a fit for me. He wore jeans and a loose shirt, and he had not shaven in three days. During the meeting he spent ten minutes lecturing me about real estate and how it works. Then, he wasted time elaborating on superfluous topics. I knew I would not be working with Wilson within the first ten minutes I met with him.

"What was my mistake?" you ask. I did not want to be rude, so I stayed for the full hour and was charged accordingly. Instead, I should have gotten up at the ten-minute mark, thanked him for his time, picked up the bill for ten minutes, and gone on my way.

I had a similar experience when I met with Joe. I walked into his office and greeted the receptionist. I waited for a few minutes and saw a man walking into a meeting room. He didn't greet anyone, nor did he scan the waiting room for clients or acknowledge the existence of any other humans in his office. I immediately felt his arrogance. Somehow, I went into the meeting room and asked if he was the lawyer I was meeting. He said, "Yes." At this moment I made the mistake of staying to speak with him for thirty minutes, when I should have left right then and there.

When he heard about my net-worth, his eyes opened wide, and he became very interested in my case. I was quite sickened that this human didn't feel I merited a simple greeting, yet as soon as he learned the potential for making money, his face lit up like a Christmas tree.

This is just one more reason why you need to go ready with questions and pay very close attention to the lawyer's body language during your conversation. If you happen to have money, and if the lawyer lights up like a Christmas tree once you disclose your net worth, then you know you have to run.

Tip: You are now in the business of getting professional legal representation. You need to be all about business and be very direct. Of course, this does not mean to be insulting, but cutting useless meetings short, leaving after a few minutes, and firing your lawyer when it's not working out is exactly what you must do.

On the other hand, once you find a lawyer to champion your case, then you must always follow up with your next actionable items and be cordial. But the lawyer must know you are interested in your own case and are diligent in following up. No human will be more interested in your case than yourself, and you must always keep your hands on the wheel.

Another lawyer I interviewed, Charles, was close to retirement. I thought his vast experience would be a real asset to my case even though he was expensive. I decided to retain him to represent me in chambers.

Being as naive as I was, I did not put enough weight to the fact that he spoke a lot about his vacation spots and the great time he had at these destinations. With hindsight as 20/20 vision, it is clear his mind was already into the next adventure. He turned out to be a disaster in chambers.

What did I fail to see?

I did not ask sufficient questions to ascertain if his passion was still in defending clients. His dreams and personal goals were more aligned toward nice vacations in hot climates—he was mostly riding the wave of a long career which enabled him to draw in enough clients to pay for his next diversion. I also failed to place enough weight on his unprofessional dressing habits, as he looked more like he was ready for a walk in the park than a lawyer meeting with a client.

When he learned I had a home and some equity in it, his eyes lit up and he smiled like he was eating a banana sideways. I had that gut feeling I should have dropped him, but again, I did not listen to my own internal voice telling me to get out.

If you notice your lawyer's eyes growing twice their normal size and a big smile appearing on their face when you disclose your net worth, I suggest you leave as fast as possible. That is all you need to know. This is why it is so important to observe and pay close attention to your lawyer's reactions and facial expressions throughout your first meeting.

When I mentioned the high cost of litigation, Charles looked at me with a sly smile and said, "Don't worry about that, there is good money coming your way." Again, I should have run right then and there. When I fired him a few weeks later, he sent me a long e-mail offering an agreement that I would not need to pay him until the family home sold. I dismissed his offer immediately.

Some say it is best to get an aggressive lawyer to handle your case, but on careful examination, one can see the danger in that advice. The only way for a lawyer to handle your case aggressively (vs. assertively) is if they are all around aggressive, meaning in the way they approach work all around.

The pressing questions become: can they separate their aggressive nature and make sure it is directed toward the other side only and not at me? Will their aggressive nature mean they will come after our family assets by instigating a trial that could be avoided? Besides, the two of you have never met before—why would they pledge allegiance to you? These questions will help you realize an aggressive lawyer is definitely a double-edged sword, and you have no idea which end you are holding.

There are just far too many divorce cases going sideways to count, but the case described below is one of many that can highlight how terrible things can go when caught unaware. It highlights many of the points I make in this book and emphasizes the very real risks I want you to be aware of and avoid at all costs. The following article titled "BC Woman May Lose Home Over

Huge Lawyer Bill" was published by the *Canadian Broadcasting Corporation* on December 2012. I include the most relevant paragraphs worth reviewing and considering:

> Woman owes $180,000 despite winning lawsuit and being awarded costs.... A B.C. woman stands to lose her home to her lawyer, who is moving to foreclose on her to pay his six-figure bill. "My friends and family say this can't be happening. There's got to be a mistake," Dale Fotsch said...."I won, but I lost," Fotsch said. "I defended myself and now I'm losing my place."...The case took nine years to resolve, which was years longer than her lawyer had predicted, she said.
>
> She said she had already paid thousands in legal fees when the case finally went to trial in 2007. As it advanced, her lawyer said he wouldn't continue unless she allowed him to secure a $100,000 mortgage against her property, at eighteen per cent interest per year.
>
> "I've done nothing wrong. What have I done wrong?" Fotsch said, choking up in tears.
>
> "I've gone to court like they told me I had to, to save my place. And now the very person that I got to help me is taking it."... "But you know, we all make mistakes. It just seems like a big price to pay." [1]

When I read this article, I could not help but wonder what kind of advice she received from friends and family. Were they all wearing nice tees? Did they advise her to get an aggressive lawyer? Did they warn her of the risks, and carefully explain how to find and work with a lawyer?

As you can see from Ms. Fotsch's experience, she did everything "right" according to what she was told. Perhaps it looked right to her friends and family as well. It is a telltale sign when her friends and family are quoted as saying "this can't be happening," indicating they were equally shocked at the outcome when it was announced. It is a tragedy no one in her circle was able to see what was coming years prior. After all, the case took nine years. What went wrong? She let go of the wheel and stopped stirring her case. Ms. Fotsch is quoted saying, "When I was hit with this, it was just like a bomb went off in my life." Makes one wonder, if the case took nine years, was she not checking regularly on what the bill was? She surrendered her power to the lawyer and lost the house. I truly feel for anyone who gets taken to the cleaners in court.

The article on Ms. Fotsch's case implies she absolutely had no other choice but to go to court and was caught unaware.

Nobody needs to know law to see that it simply does not make sense for a case of this kind to drag on for so long. I can say the legal system has improved marginally since this case came to light, but the potential for someone to end up in the same situation is most definitely still there.

One thing is clear, Ms. Fotsch had no idea of the implications of the agreement she signed with her lawyer. She placed all her trust in him, thinking he was there to protect her rights. It is possible she was advised to get an aggressive lawyer. To gain insight into aggressive business practices, I recommend watching the movie, *The Founder*, with Michael Keaton. Remember, lawyers are business people.

Had I listened to and kept Charles in retainer, I could possibly have ended up in the same situation as Ms. Fotsch.

How Much Will It Cost?

The question everyone wants to know the answer to is, "How much will my divorce cost?" The answer is, "How long is a string?" It is just not possible to say, there are just way too many variables. Every divorce should be completed on a one-thousand to five-thousand dollar budget, but anger and resentment, can easily drive it to several hundreds of thousands of dollars and make it drag on for years. It only takes one lawyer to inundate the other side with e-mails, requests, and demands, drawing both sides into a never-ending correspondence cycle. A three-page letter can easily cost $350 or more and not get you any closer to a solution.

Unless there are some particular reasons I am not aware of, it is important to set a seven-day trial at the onset of your case and make sure there is an end to what could easily become a never-ending correspondence chain of $350 letters. If you have kids and a family home and mediation is not agreed upon, then trial may be the best, or only, solution. Judges prefer to solve the issue of parenting and asset division at trial. If there is no history of family violence or criminal records, then in all likelihood your divorce can be handled in summary trial, much cheaper than a seven-day trial, and a little easier to self-represent.

CHAPTER 3

Preparing Yourself

The purpose of getting a lawyer is not to win. The word "win" in family court is actually a misnomer because the moment you retain a lawyer you start losing. The reason you are going to court is to potentially lose less than what you would if you didn't.

A bad marriage with a problem that used to belong to two people now belongs to four, and five, if you count the judge, by the time you go to court! Prior to starting this process, you only had your ex to deal with. After the process starts, you have your lawyer and the lawyer for the other side to deal with. How much better do you think it gets when there are two complete strangers in the mix?

What you and your ex deserve is an equal division of assets and equal parenting time. This is fair. Most often than not, if you are commencing the litigation process, it is because one or perhaps both of you, is trying to keep as much as possible—good old fashioned anger, resentment, and revenge. Most of the time this is what family litigation is all about, one trying to get something over on the other.

At this juncture in life, you want to end your divorce as fast as possible with the least amount of emotional turmoil and meltdowns. Entering the family law machine will turn two spouses into court combatants and set ablaze any trace of friendly communications, eat the family savings, and inflict even more damage on the children. It is hard to justify the fallout that trial ensues in exchange of a sweet sense of revenge for the combative spouse. After all, everything comes with its own karma price.

This may sound like an aphorism because it is. Any efforts in destroying an ex will only result in emotional and financial harm to everyone. Court litigation is the one place where the winner also loses.

This is even more relevant if you have children. After divorcing, you will want to keep some level of civility with your ex to keep raising your kids. Remember, you are divorcing your spouse, but there is no way of divorcing your children.

One of the darkest tragedies is the emotional destruction a high conflict, litigious divorce inflicts on the children involved. Generally, one parent, sometimes both parents, will not hesitate to use the children as go-to weapons to inflict damage onto the other, turning children into cannon fodder to fire at the other side. The horror stories of children caught up in the middle of parental warfare are just too many to mention. This problem is so palpable in society that it is probably close to impossible to grasp the extent of it all. Manipulating children to take sides is really a terrible thing to do, and yet there seems to be no solution in sight for protecting children in litigious divorces.

You also have to plan for the future. Chances are you may need your ex's help one day. Life happens, and the future is uncertain. Nobody knows whose help will be needed in the future. It just makes sense to keep things civil and amicable, especially when there are children from the marriage. Life will not be easy after waging war in the courtroom.

WARNING: Homework up ahead! Before and during your legal journey you must read up on family law and learn all you can about it. Your first assignment is to read and have some level of understanding of family law as per your state or province.

- ✓ A good place to start is https://www.supremecourtbc.ca/family-law
- ✓ And the Family Law Act https://www.bclaws.gov.bc.ca/civix/document/id/complete/statreg/11025_00

A good place to start in the family law act is Part 5 – Property Division, Division 1 General Rules which states:

Equal Entitlement and Responsibility

81-Subject to an agreement or order that provides otherwise and except as set out in this Part and Part 6 *[Pension Division]*,

- a) Spouses are both entitled to family property and responsible for family debt, regardless of their respective use or contribution, and
- b) On separation, each spouse has a right to an undivided half interest in all family property as a tenant in common and is equally responsible for family debt.

No matter what someone may suggest, you are entitled to your fifty percent share of assets of the marriage. This is your starting point.

Let's say that negotiation with your ex is such that your spouse is willing to sign the divorce papers if she gets fifty-five percent of the assets. You may really want to consider it. That extra five percent may still be less than the cost and headache of litigating in court. A seven-day trial will be upwards of $70,000 when fully represented. A two-day summary trial will be upwards of $15,000, and the headache. These are some numbers to consider when deciding on your bottom line in negotiations.

At this point I feel compelled to share what happened with a good friend who divorced a narcissist during the time she was being treated for cancer. To this day I have no idea how she was able to deal with two of the fiercest challenges in life (for anyone) at the same time—treating a malignant tumor and dealing with a narcissist who wanted to take her to the cleaners.

In the end, her ex lost respect in the community, as well as all chances of maintaining a cordial conversation with the mother of his children. She never gave up, persevered, and received a fair settlement.

Divorce Goals

- ✓ Reach a fair settlement.
- ✓ Do it in the most amicable way possible.
- ✓ Complete in the shortest amount of time possible.

Simple right? Easier said than done. For some very strange reason, it was not until almost two years later that my lawyer, Michael, made a strong argument regarding point number three, to finish it as soon as possible (have an end date). Why was I not told that before?

There is nothing worse than prolonging a conflict unnecessarily. If divorce is unavoidable, then you really want to do it in as short time as possible and avoid dragging it out for years. When looking back into my case, my second lawyer should have sent a letter similar to this:

> "We would really like to find a settlement through the most amicable way possible either through collaboration or mediation, and we feel confident we can do so. In order to make sure we work our hardest to reach a

friendly settlement in short order, we want to schedule a full seven-day trial. Please provide us your available dates for trial a year from now."

Granted, at that stage I was not even ready to hear the word trial, but my lawyer should have sat me down for an hour and explained to me carefully the strategic importance of having a trial date. Chances are good, a lawyer will not take the time to carefully explain why things need to be done in a certain way, and you don't know what you don't know.

Book a seven-day trial early in the process. The trial should be one-year out. The point of making this booking is to make sure there is an end to it all. You will use this year to see if there is any way to settle out of court, and the trial date is the incentive for everyone to work within that time frame. Remember Ms. Fotsch's case mentioned above? It took nine years to resolve in court. Even if she had not been taken to the cleaners by her own lawyer (which was already bad enough), she had to endure this process for nine full years. I cannot fathom.

It took me four years to arrive at my summary trial as self-represented, and that was extraordinarily long and painful. Hence my writing this book to help you avoid the same mistakes many of us make.

One year is long enough time to settle, that is if there is at least some will on both sides to want to settle out of court. A final trial date is a tremendous incentive to want to settle out of court before the date arrives.

I would like to offer a word of caution: It is highly encouraged to refrain from having another relationship while in the divorce process, even when both agree it is time to divorce, or perhaps particularly when both agree to divorce, and mediation is a possibility. There have been cases where both agree to go to mediation only for one to find out the other has already started a relationship. That is enough to spark the vengeful fires of litigation. The risk is just too high.

What happens if you never settle in a friendly way? You can still attempt to resolve in a two-day summary trial (if your case is not overly complicated, that is). If you end up in a seven-day trial, then you would have done everything possible to avoid it, and it was simply not possible.

A seven-day trial with full representation can cost upwards of $70,000, and this is the reason I (and most people) wanted to avoid it at all costs. It turns out that I ended up losing a lot by the wayward path I took in litigation. Again, no one lawyer sat me down and explained it straight to me. No one took time from the get-go to explain that if the other side failed to negotiate, a trial was the only solution for me. I was also very stubborn and did not want to hear the word trial. I did not even want to consider hearing, and yet that is exactly what I needed to hear from the start.

In the highly likely event that you do not have the money for full representation, then try unbundled services, and if that does not work try pro-bono. Unbundled is far better than having no legal advice at all. Unbundled services and self-representing are a huge amount of work. In fact, it is like having a second full-time job. It is far from easy, but if this is what you have to do, then this is what you have to do. I spent over 150 hours preparing for my two-day summary trial.

As a very last resort, if you cannot afford unbundled legal help, or do not qualify for pro-bono, then you may wish to consider attending trial as a Self-Represented Litigant (SRL). I attended as an audience member in a seven-day trial where one spouse was SRL to understand what a trial is like and how it is done. SRL is not ideal, but if it comes to it, a trial will bring an end to a long drawn-out divorce, and you will have your chance to speak in front of the judge and tell your story. This is potentially much better than nothing at all. The entire process is a very big gamble indeed.

At the trial I attended, the husband had not delivered his financial statements, so the judge had to adjourn the case on day two as he could not allow the trial to proceed without full documentation.

Make sure that all documents required by the court are submitted and in front of the judge. It is damaging to everyone involved to be at trial, expecting to finalize the case in the next seven days, only to hear the judge say he does not have all the information. Then, the court has to adjourn for months, and the trial begins again when everything is in order and properly submitted.

The psychological and financial toll on delays like this is simply too much. Do everything necessary to bring closure to a divorce in the shortest amount of time. In his book, *The Art of War*, Sun Tzu clearly says wars must never be prolonged. [2]

Dealing with Fear

At the beginning of this book, I mentioned how completely scared of going to court I was and dreaded the mere thought of it. One of the reasons we hold on to fear is that we all have heard horror stories coming out from the family court system. However, we never hear of the divorce trials that ended in fair and equitable judgements handled by level-headed lawyers and judges. The truth is there are many like that. Your job is to put in the best effort possible to find the lawyer who will partner with you and make an honest effort to advocate on your behalf.

At one point I learned to accept the process and began reading all the material I could about it.

I found that preparing for litigation is about reading, writing, preparing, filing, and archiving, all activities I like doing, so I was able to do a reasonable job in preparing my case. Why was I so afraid in the beginning? I was afraid of the unknown. I had no idea what to expect.

The purpose of this book is to help you deal with fear by helping you formulate a road map to your case. Yes, you can get through your divorce keeping your sanity and good health.

If you are headed to trial then it really makes sense to take the time to attend other divorce trials. They are public, so anyone can attend. You will see that most litigants in Supreme Court are fully represented, and there is simply no unruly behaviour or rude talking. Those movie scenes where a lawyer screams at a witness and spit comes out of their mouth do not really exist. You will also see that lawyers mostly read from their documents. It is easier to appreciate that once all documents are prepared and filed. You can also read them in front of a judge.

Once I attended (as an audience) a trial with a self-represented litigant. I found myself saying, "If he can do it, so can I."

Keep in mind that due to the exorbitant costs of litigation, Self-Represented Litigants or SRLs are on the rise, and more and more people go at it alone. The courts recognize this trend, and judges are more accepting of SRLs than before. When going to court, remember to dress up. Do not wear a tee.

I believe this is important enough that it merits repeating. We have all heard horror divorce stories and know the system is broken, but not all is lost. There are definitely good lawyers and good judges out there. We never hear about the divorce trials that ended up in fair and balanced judgements, because there is not much excitement in those stories. But they do happen, so keep your spirits high and be convinced that you will get the legal help to do the right thing for you.

The following is an inspirational writing by Seema M. Dewan, prolific author of various books on spiritual wisdom, which I find very suitable to close this section. In fact you will notice every section closes with her writings, which I took from her Facebook page titled "Inspirational writings by Seema M Dewan."

Higher Thinking

Everything depends on how you think…what thoughts you allow yourself to be led by…which thoughts you filter…which thoughts become a part of your personality…which thoughts determine your character…

We often feel the ruling thought in us must be to save ourselves. But we seldom save ourselves. We attempt to save what we desire so much. We begin to think we are the desire. With that, we make many mistakes. And mistakes lead to misunderstanding ourselves and carrying us to a world of fears.

We feel that fear follows us. But that's not true. We are the ones that follow our fears. We think that the more we think of our fears, the more the fears will be lessened. But that's a myth. We have to not think and foster our fears. If we think them, we must learn to remove them completely and fully from our minds.

It is not difficult to face our fears. It is much more difficult to foster them. We reflect on our fears only because we have given so much understanding to our fears. Our biggest fear is to face our fears and uproot them. It is that fear we have to face boldly without any reservations.

We fear what others think of us. But what do we think of ourselves? That's most important. We often think if others cannot see the weakness in us, we are going to be okay. But are we okay? Are we happy simply knowing that others are blinded by our superficial nature? To face our fears, we need to stand by truth. Only if we are truthful to ourselves will fears dwindle. Hence, choose seeing the truth within you rather than covering the deception of following untruth.

We often say it's not easy to remove the fears within us. Really? Who is saying that it's not easy? It's just the fear of being defiant of facing truth. We often say, "Why change anything… when things are pushing along? Why change ourselves when we have understood the reasons why we fear? Why upturn the boat when the passengers in this boat think just like me?" We often think, "I am not the only one falling!" But that does matter? First save yourself. Then others too will be saved.

We want to change ourselves without changing anything. We fear knowing who we have been all these years. It takes one moment of sincerity to change everything that one has resented and repented about one's mistakes.

One moment that says, "That's enough…I will begin my change no matter what it takes."

One moment that says, "Why am I not believing in myself to make this change?"

One moment that says, "Stop this way of petty thinking…I am from now making every moment worthwhile by being the self I respect."

Yes! Respecting yourself is everything. It's the greatest gift to yourself.

Begin anew. Think courage over fear…think patience over anger…think peace over confrontation…think righteousness over selfishness…think love over hatred…think effort over ease...think giving over wanting...think unity over division...think friendship over war...think a smile over a frown...think understanding over judgement...think wisdom over aggression...think duty over desire...and think faith over doubt.

This is the moment...we all begin anew....carrying the truth...and tossing away the voice of fear within us. [3]

SECTION II

The Process

CHAPTER 4

Roadmap

I briefly touched on this before—now it is time to expand a little on each of the available paths to resolution and peripheral points of information:
- ✓ Negotiation
- ✓ Mediation
- ✓ Collaborative Divorce
- ✓ Arbitration
- ✓ Summary Trial
- ✓ Seven- to Ten-day Trial
- ✓ Piecemeal Court Applications

Remember, there are also different options for having representation including: full representation, unbundled, pro bono, or no legal help. Even with no legal help, there is much you can do to present your case in court. Do not give up—it's not easy, but not impossible either.

Negotiation

In a negotiation, you and your ex draw up your very own separation agreement, sign it, and move your merry way. It may be rare, but it happens. Just make sure to sign and validate it. If you can manage to settle your affairs through this process, then throw this book into the fire or better yet, donate it to someone who needs it.

Mediation

When using mediation, you agree on most items but there are a few points of disagreement. Hiring a mediator will help you iron out the final details, sign, and be on your merry way. I hope this one works out for you. It is possible to work with just one mediator without lawyers if you get a good mediator.

Collaborative Divorce

In a collaborative divorce, each person hires a lawyer, and the lawyers negotiate on behalf of each spouse. Much risk appears at this stage, particularly if there is a significant asset base in the family. It only takes one aggressive lawyer to drag the entire case to trial. I recommend watching *Liar Liar* with Jim Carey, as it is a very good depiction of what can happen.

Mediation Plus Each Has a Lawyer

If there are strong indications that mediation will help you settle, then it is your obligation to do so. Every chance to settle in the most amicable way must be given a strong consideration. Missing a genuine opportunity to resolve divorce in mediation would be **tragic**.

Word of caution:

> Do not be pressured into signing anything until you have had a chance to review it thoroughly.

Yes, there is such a thing as mediation settlement regret, when later you find out you signed something you did not completely understand. Also, remember the work and effort you put into mediation does not carry over to court in case there is no agreement. In other words, if mediation is unsuccessful, then all the work and money is for naught.

A good lawyer should have a pretty good idea if mediation has any chances based on a few e-mail exchanges with the other side. For starters, the two lawyers should be able to either agree or come close to agreement on division of assets and parenting time. If the two lawyers are miles apart on these two items, the chances of successful mediation are pretty low.

You can easily spend upwards of $5,000 in mediation, and it may take several months to get there. If mediation is not successful, not only have you wasted your time and money, you will have wasted all that preparation. Hardly any documents you present in mediation can be presented in court. It is not like you can take the same stack of papers to advance your case in trial. Trial in court is a completely different stage with very strict rules for presentation of submissions. Perhaps there is a possibility that a small amount of the documentation could be reused in court, so you have to be very smart and strategic in deciding if you want to mediate or not.

One lawyer told me that he had walked into mediations where he was surprised it actually worked and a divorce agreement was drawn up and signed. While embarking on your journey, every decision is a risk. When doing anything, you really need to have a strong sense of the risk/cost/benefit scenario.

In the case of mediation, you really need some indication of success. Going into it just to see if it works is too costly and burns lots of time and effort. It is far better to spend one hour in consultation with the lawyer discerning the real risk/cost/benefit of any decision than to spend several thousand dollars later without proper understanding and seeing its potential failure.

If you are not communicating with your ex and your respective lawyers are not seeing eye to eye on what a fair separation agreement looks like, then it is highly likely mediation will be a waste of time and money for you. Your respective lawyers must either agree or come close to agreeing on what division of assets and parenting time looks like to move on with mediation, for it to work. Remember, the mediator cannot make a judgement and cannot impose any orders—it is up to the spouses to agree.

The key to your case is seeing and accepting reality as it is, whether that takes the form of mediation or a full-blown trial. Denying one's reality is a terrible foe.

The other side offered to mediate while I was being fully represented by Bob, who tried to convince me to agree to mediation. After the first experience, I knew in my bones he was giving me wrong advice. Also, the opposite side had shown their colours and demonstrated to be highly aggressive. Bob kept minimizing their aggressions as if they were not there, and I was beginning to feel controlled. I wondered how he could not simply see the other side was aggressive and was not really interested in meaningful negotiations. I refused mediation being fully represented, as he would have taken months to prepare, and I would have had to pay upwards of $5,000.

Bob kept taking a long time to complete actionable items, anywhere from one to three weeks for simple letters. I kept putting pressure to get things done, up until the time when he fired himself. Firing himself turned out to be a blessing in disguise, as he was not representing my best interests anymore.

After Bob, I went into unbundled self-representation with Michael. After much conversation, Michael convinced me I should give mediation a try. This time I agreed because I would only spend a thousand dollars in trying it out, as self-represented. By that time, I knew so much about my own case that I had the confidence to go to mediation without a lawyer.

Looking back, this, too, was a mistake as I knew mediation was a waste of time, but my lawyer said it was a good idea to try. This is your reminder that you must be at the wheel of your case and always steer it in the direction you see fit.

There are those times that even when it is painfully obvious that mediation is a complete waste of time, lawyers will still recommend it, just because it is the thing to do. Always be asking what the risk benefit is of doing something. If it turns out to be a waste of time, just as you thought, then it is indeed a waste of time and money. By now hopefully you have already set up a full trial, so you have an end date to work toward.

I found it was very difficult to qualify a mediator as I could not find any information on them and their success. I pretty much had to roll the dice and put forward three names. Turns out the one I selected was rather weak as he did not know anything about family law. While in mediation, he tried hard to convince me to settle for a terrible deal. The mediator got really frustrated that I kept rejecting his proposal, and he even tried to convince me the other side had a strong case, when in fact I knew they did not.

You need a very strong mediator, who preferably is also a lawyer, and understands what is fair, and is willing to knock some sense into both of you.

Hands down, the best advice I can give you: prepare, prepare, prepare. Always prepare before going to any resolution meeting. Provide full disclosure and write down all the relevant aspects of your case and proposed outcome. Your preparation should be so thorough that you can simply read off of your documents. You do not want to commit anything to memory, because you will forget, especially when under pressure.

Before mediation you should write a document called the mediation brief. Below I have included a sample mediation brief, which closely resembles what I submitted although the names, dates, and numbers have been changed. As you can see, it is pretty descriptive and leaves nothing to memory. When I went into mediation, I was able to simply read off my brief and state my position, which went according to family law guidelines.

WITHOUT PREJUDICE – FOR MEDIATION ONLY

Claimant: Oscar
Respondent: Joanne

MEDIATION BRIEF OF THE CLAIMANT – OSCAR

Date: September 1, 2020
Mediator: Joe Smith
Parties: Oscar   Counsel: John Doe
                Joanne   Counsel: Jane Doe

PARTIES

1. The Claimant, Oscar, was born on November 3, 1998. He is currently twenty-four years old.

2. The Respondent, Joanne, was born on December 5, 2000. She is currently twenty-two years old.
3. The parties are the natural parents of two children:
Billi, born Jan 23, 2004;
Sandy, born Jan 24, 2004;
(Collectively, the "Children")
4. The parties were married on January 1, 2005.
5. There is a dispute about the date of separation. The parties' positions are as follows:
Mr. Oscar: November 24, 2017
Ms. Joanne: November 20, 2018
6. The parties have lived in the property located at *address*. The parties continue to reside in the Former Family Home with the Children to the present date.

ISSUES

7. The issues are:
   a) parenting arrangements;
   b) child support;
   c) spousal support; and
   d) Division of family property and debt

PROCEDURAL HISTORY

8. March 1915 – I moved out
9. Etc.
10. etc.

MR. OSCAR'S POSITION

Parenting arrangements

11. *Parenting time*: I seek an equal parenting time schedule with the Children, which I firmly believe is in the Children's best interests. I believe a "week-on, week-off" schedule would be ideal for both the parties and the Children, but I am also open to discussing the possibility of other equal parenting time schedules.
12. I have been an active and involved father to the Children throughout their lives.
13. *Parental responsibilities*: My proposed terms are as follows:
    a) The parties are guardians of the Children pursuant to the *Family Law Act*.
    b) The parties will equally share all of the s. 41 parental responsibilities for the Children pursuant to s. 40(2) of the *Family Law Act*.
    c) The parties will discuss significant decisions regarding the Children with each other and will have the obligation to try to reach agreement on those decisions.
    d) In the event that the parties cannot reach agreement regarding a significant decision despite their best efforts, either party will be at liberty to apply to court pursuant to s. 49 of the *Family Law Act*.

Child support

14. I have a 2020 Guideline income of $60,790 in employment income.

15. I claim that Ms. Joanne's income should be $20,000.
16. Based on a Guideline income of $60,790 for me and $20,000 for Ms. Joanne, pursuant to section 9 of the *Federal Child Support Guidelines*:
    a) Mr. Oscar should pay Ms. Joanne $1,000
17. *Section 7 expenses:* describe ongoing child expenses

Spousal support

18. For the purposes of settlement, I agree using a separation date of November 20, 2018 to calculate spousal support obligations.
19. On November 13, 2018, I sent an e-mail I want out.
20. Using the incomes for each party noted above, I offer to pay $xxx.xx per month in spousal support for 10 years (see attached DivorceMate calculations).

Division of family property and debt

21. As with the issue of spousal support, for the purposes of settlement, I am agreeable to using a separation date of November 20, 2018 to determine the division of family property and debt.
22. I seek an equal division of family property and debt. I do not raise any excluded property claims.
23. The primary asset is the Former Family Home. Ms. Joanne has expressed an interest in retaining the Former Family Home in the division of family property and debt.
24. I am open to discussing a potential division of family property and debt that would allow Ms. Joanne to remain in the Former Family Home.

25. The following additional information is required in order to determine an equal division:
   a) List all documents missing from the other side

Other

26. List other outstanding items

ALL OF WHICH IS RESPECTFULLY SUBMITTED.

_____   _____

Dated September 1, 2020   Oscar

    The last thing you want to do is go in empty-handed and stutter your way through, not knowing what you want, what you are entitled to, and worst of all, not knowing what a fair settlement is.

    Again, many people end up settling for completely unfair deals, because they wanted out so quick, were distraught, and end up signing settlements that were simply not right, only to have deep regrets about it for many years.

    As mentioned in previous pages, just because you are the paying customer, does not mean the service provider has your best interest at heart. Remember, true genuine allegiances cannot be bought, they must be searched, validated, and finally retained. Below is a review I found on Google Maps of a mediator and describes how things can go wrong when attending a session unprepared and with the wrong human.

    The following is a Google Maps review of a mediator.

> "Terrible experience. Ms. ... cares about her track record for 'settling' cases at all costs. She is warm and personable and easy to talk to. She got to know me and then

used my weaknesses against me to 'close the deal' with high pressure and emotional mind games. I was kept alone in a different room and not allowed to participate in the discussions. My ex and I were sold different versions of the settlement agreement arriving at the same numbers (apparently this is not uncommon - but sets up a lifetime of resentment and misunderstanding). Without my knowing she let my ex's lawyer type changes to part of the agreement that had already been decided (I did not know to re-read those parts). Emotionally and financially the single biggest mistake of my life."

Anecdotally speaking, I have a friend who would echo these same words.

Again: prepare, prepare, prepare.

If everything is in place and you know what you are doing, then the outcome should be this:

Another mediator review from Google Maps

"Stephanie is a great mediator. I just went through a difficult separation and we used Stephanie to attempt mediation. She talked to the two of us separately to understand our point of view, our starting points and our areas of concern when trying to find an agreement.

When all together we worked out the issues that were amicable. When we hit a contentious topic, she did not allow us to bicker and separated us to discuss the matter with each of us individually and come to a compromise without an argument.

We came to a signed settlement within 3 months of separation. I feel the process found a fair compromise within a very short time frame and avoided the costs and stresses of going to court.

All in all I would recommend Stephanie as an effective mediator and I am very happy she was able to help us through such a difficult process."

Hopefully your situation is one that can be solved in mediation. Placing the right value on mediation is one of the trickiest things to do in this process.

In early stages of my case, after much haggling and discussion with my lawyer, Julian initially convinced the opposite side to agree to mediation, to the point that I offered to pay in full for the mediator just to make things easy. I was adamant to avoid trial and solve our divorce through mediation, as I knew this was the most sensible thing to do.

Here's another one of my big mistakes: both people must pay for their share of mediation, because both people must have skin in the game. Both parties must show interest in resolving the issue as soon as possible, as cost effective as possible. When I paid for the mediation in full, it showed that only I was interested in a solution, but I could not see this at the time. I had tunnel vision, and all I wanted to see was an end as soon as possible—I was not able to appreciate the psychology of proper process.

One day before mediation, the other side cancelled, without any explanation whatsoever. My lawyer had spent countless hours preparing for it, and we were both very frustrated. I had to swallow the fact that I had just wasted a ton of money and time in preparation for it.

The reality of the situation is that some lawyers will recommend mediation even when it is painfully clear it will not work. It seems to be a question of simple math sometimes where your lawyer is being paid an hourly rate, no matter what type of resolution he is trying to accomplish on your behalf. So if you go to mediation and it fails, then you have just paid for that event, plus all the upcoming litigation to go to court.

There is also the other side of the coin to consider: there are most definitely those situations when your case is perfectly suitable for mediation, and instead, your lawyer will push for trial. These are the extremely difficult decisions you are confronted with every step of the way; every decision is strategically important.

Julian mentioned he had been to mediations that were likely to fail and yet it was successful, and other sessions that were likely to succeed, yet failed. I propose this is not a good strategy. You need to ascertain your real chances of success prior to mediation. Some indications of success are:

- ✓ Both agree to mediate
- ✓ Both will pay their half of the mediator
- ✓ Both are interested in closure and getting on with life
- ✓ Both have a similar understanding of what a fair divorce looks like

If you have to jump through hoops and spend an enormous amount of time and effort to convince the other side to mediate, then your chances of success are slim. However, maybe your ex just hired an assertive and not an aggressive lawyer. If that is the case, your lucky stars are smiling down at you, because an assertive lawyer will explain what a fair separation agreement is and will help you both settle in the most amicable way possible.

You will know where you stand by the tone of the e-mails being exchanged between lawyers.

If you happen to receive strong recommendations about a particular mediator who is known to be tough, fair, and knowledgeable, then they are your person. I thought all mediators had a legal background, but it turns out this is not the case, so make sure yours does.

Mediation - Arbitration

Mediation – Arbitration is a great way to resolve your conflict outside the public eye and have some sense of control of the process.

In this case, if mediation does not solve your issues, you can agree to let an arbitrator decide for you. The arbitrator pronounces a judgement for you which is as valid as that of a judge in court. You have to pay the costs of the mediator and arbitrator, but it is more expedient and efficient than mediation alone.

Had the other side accepted this option I would have jumped on it right away. It allows you to resolve your issues faster, privately, and you can choose your arbitrator, which means you can search for an arbitrator who has plenty of experience in family law. You may know that in the court system you get whichever judge is assigned to your case, and you have no idea who you are going to get until the morning you show up. The judge may have lots of experience in corporate law and very little in family law. Suddenly they get to decide your case.

Summary Trial

If you need to go to court and there is no record of violence and your finances are relatively straightforward, then summary trial may be your best alternative.

This is a one- or two-day long chambers where your case is resolved through Affidavits and you or your lawyer get to present your case in front of the judge. This is the best way to go to trial and the last hope of solving your case before having to go to a full seven- to ten-day trial.

In my case I did not know anything about summary trials until roughly one year after I started the process. My lawyer, Bob, told me about it and arbitration during my third month working with him. Why no one told me about this before I cannot understand, but reinforces the importance of drawing a road map at the onset and the need to be at the wheel of your case!

As I mentioned earlier, no one is going to care more about your case and its outcome than you will, so you owe it to yourself to learn all the forms of conflict resolutions. Personally, I'm stumped why lawyers don't automatically inform you of all the tools available. It may be as simple as your lawyer not believing in a particular form of resolution. For example, some feel that summary trial is simply not effective and don't even bother discussing this option with clients. Again, you need to be aware of these options and understand their benefits as potential options.

I was a SRL in my two-day summary trial through Michael's unbundled legal services. Michael was a young and very bright lawyer with experience in litigation. He was instrumental in directing my efforts to produce all the required documents for me to represent myself in court.

If you are in a position to cover full representation, then I highly recommend this option. As mentioned earlier, SRL is the equivalent of having a full-time second job. Over the span of two months, I spent upwards of 150 hours putting together my case. I worked on my case every hour when I was not at work. It is not an undertaking for the faint of heart, as it really was an enormous amount of work.

This is a picture of the documents I prepared for my summary trial. As you can see, this is a stack of documents five inches high, and around 1,300 sheets of paper, printed single-sided.

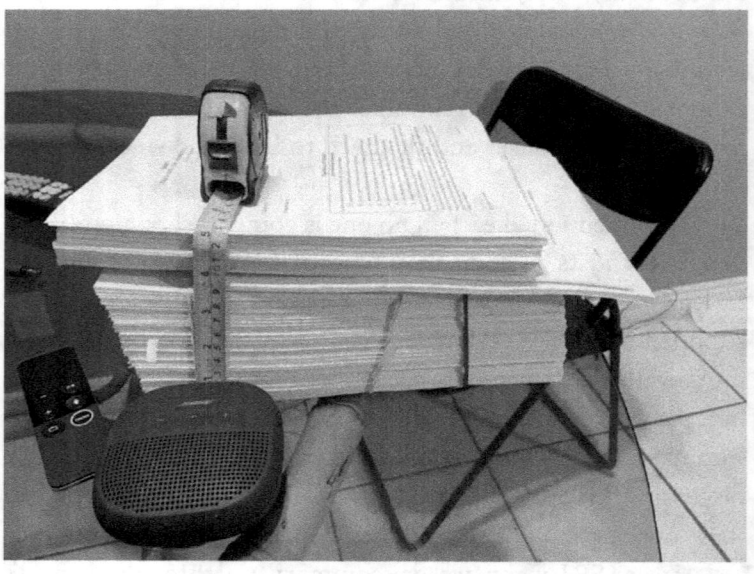

Yes, for some reason, all submissions to court for trial must be printed single-sided. Don't ask me why, those are the rules.

I still have the same speaker, TV, music subscription, and measuring tape, by the way. I cannot recommend enough working with some good music in the background. You will need some mental clarity while producing your paperwork.

After printing the original work, I then had to produce two copies—two for the opposite side and the original for the court, I did not print one for me. That is close to 4,000 sheets of paper all together. I am not counting the wasted 2,000 sheets of paper I had to print during the course of litigation.

For the trial date I did not print a full set of summary trial documents; I only printed a few sheets for myself, and the rest I referenced from my soft copies on my computer during trial. One of the documents I printed included my written submissions, as I practically read from them. Apparently, judges don't like it when someone just reads off the paper, but that is the best I could do. When I got to speak on the second day, I addressed several false accusations from the other side as all presented evidence on my documents.

Also, I believe I could have used the same documents had I gone to a full trial. At the very least, had I been SRL on a full trial, those same documents would have at least provided me enough material to put up a reasonable case.

The court had implemented the new remote protocols for chambers due to COVID-19, and unfortunately, I had to represent myself remotely through the phone only. This was a huge drawback as you lose a lot of information by not being present. It really was a challenging environment to deal with.

As I came to understand it, written submissions are not mandatory in a summary trial, but for myself as a self-represented litigant, I can say I would have been dead in the water without them. I simply read my case from the written submissions. If you are SRL, I would highly encourage you to have yours included in your court documents.

If you are in the process of preparing your own case, I highly recommend using Microsoft Office and Adobe Acrobat. Once all documents are completed in Microsoft Word, they have to be put into a single PDF file— it is the easiest way to manage your pleadings. Acrobat PDF is the application that gives you all the required tools to number, edit, and organize your files the way the court demands. Since you can rent this software on a monthly basis, you will only pay for the time you really need it, which will likely be two to six months. Money spent on good software is money well spent.

Seven- to Ten-day Full Trial (I hope you don't get to this)

If there is simply no way to avoid this, well at least you tried the other more "friendly" dispute resolutions.

Let's say your house is on fire and you only have a couple of minutes to get out. You will only take your most important valuables, get your kids, and run for your life, would you not? Now picture this: a firefighter comes to your rescue with oxygen tank in hand, face mask, and everything you need to get out alive. However, the firefighter demands you first answer ten skill testing questions before he can really help, and if you fail, too bad so sad, the firefighter takes your wallet and leaves you behind to burn. Feeling the warm fuzzies yet? Trial is not far from it.

Of all case filings, only 5% or so end up in full trial. Most reasonable people understand that the emotional/psychological/financial cost is just absolutely not worth it, so if anything, this statistic will help you sleep better at night, knowing the odds are in your favor, and you will likely not go to trial. In my case, I ended in summary trial, one step down from the absolute highest conflict litigation which is a seven to ten-day trial.

Litigations are tremendously adversarial. Couples in court usually end up losing whatever shreds had existed of a friendly relationship. Court litigation will ensure that absolutely no relationship is left between the two battling litigants. Very much like gladiators of the old days, I highly doubt opposing gladiators would get together in the bar for some drinks after the battle.

I honestly believe most lawyers actually do want speedy resolution. All twelve lawyers I visited were quite busy, with no lack of customers. So by and large, most lawyers do **not** need to drag out any case longer than necessary. But remember, it only takes one bad apple on either side for things to go south and go south hard and fast.

Piecemeal Court Applications

There are lawyers who prefer to solve cases via piecemeal chambers applications. They will go to chambers a number of times to ask for certain concessions each time. I had limited experience with this particular technique, but my lawyer, Michael, advised against it. I was told that more often than not, judges like to resolve all issues in one trial particularly and especially when parenting time and the sale of the family home must be determined, be it a summary or full trial.

In my case I had a house to sell (for proper division of assets) and parenting time to argue at the same two-day summary trial. Going to court to exclusively argue division of assets was close to impossible. Piecemeal chambers applications were simply not the right path for me, and most likely, it is not for you if you are in a similar situation.

There is also another danger to this process—either lawyer can simply say they are busy or on vacation to avoid giving available days to go to court. They don't need to offer any other explanation, and this way they can postpone a court appearance for many months. Having a seven-day trial booked in advance becomes the only incentive for both parties to resolve the divorce in the friendliest and cheapest way possible.

Your Most Likely Path

While it is not completely possible to predict what path your journey will take, it is fair to say that if you keep vigilant and keep asking questions, you will get a fairly good sense of which way your case will go.

Negotiation/Mediation is possible if you both are in agreement of divorce and are on talking terms. If the screaming matches still continue, then it's not looking good.

Arbitration or trial will likely happen if you experience some of the following in your relationship: screaming, guilt tripping, lying, manipulation, gaslighting, constant contradictions, shaming, blaming, dismissiveness, regular invasion of personal boundaries, playing victim, or your spouse refuses to accept divorce. These personality traits tend to appear in bundles and hardly ever just one. To the degree you find them in your marriage mirrors the degree litigation will occur.

As you begin to determine your most likely path, let me close this chapter with these incredible words from Seema M Dewan—a great lesson for all of us to take away and a state of mind to strive for.

Walking Toward Peace

The principles you uphold in your thoughts and the values you uphold in your character will give you courage and continuous strength. That courage and inner strength results in peace.

Peace is not the outcome when things go perfect for you. On the contrary peace is most experienced when you battle hard to stay rooted in what's right.

The easiest ways one takes in life results in restlessness and inner aggression. Engage all your energy in working very hard. The joy of hard work itself results in an inner silence. It forgoes the expectation to receive. That leads to a stillness of peace.

When there is a difference in the wavelength of thinking two individuals, they begin to hurt themselves and hurt each other. In every relationship there is first a misunderstanding of one's own understanding. Then only one misunderstands another. Misunderstanding of one's own nature leads to pain in a relationship.

No two individuals are perfect for each other. That's because each one's thoughts changes from time to time. It is when they come to a common way of thinking that they get along best. Think truth at all times. The truth will always guide you to a better self. Even if another does not agree with you…you can still understand why another misunderstands you. That will lead to peace.

Patience is the power of peace. Do not be in a hurry to respond to any matter. The urgency to respond has a whisper of failure itself. Wait till your mind thinks logically and is not encased in fear to rush. Everything happens at the right time. That which is truth today will be truth tomorrow too. Wait… be confident…be calm. Then translate your thought into action. That action will not hurt you nor any other.

The moment you complain you shall lose your peace. To talk of others' mistakes is the biggest mistake. It's like saying, "I am standing in line to do what's wrong, but I am last in the line. Hence I am better than the ones who stand before me." You may be the last in line to make a mistake, but you will also be making more mistakes as you watch others making mistakes and talking about their downfalls. You will also be the last to realize your weaknesses. Hence standalone...watch yourself with the intensity to transform. Peace is cleansing your mind...your wrong intentions...your false pride...your inner aggression...your dislikes...your petty impressions...your huge expectations...and your pompous visions of others being good.

Making peace begins with being at peace." [4]

SECTION III

Technical Elements

CHAPTER 5

Case Description

Now that we covered the different modes of resolution, we can speak to some legal technical elements that may or may not be part of your experience.
- ✓ JCC - Judicial Case Conference
- ✓ Retainers
- ✓ Separation Date
- ✓ DM - DivorceMate Calculations
- ✓ Documentation
- ✓ Views of the Child Report - Section 211
- ✓ Counselling
- ✓ False Criminal Charges
- ✓ Parental Alienation

JCC - Judicial Case Conference

According to the "Family Legal Aid" website, the definition of JCC is as follows:

> "A Judicial Case Conference (JCC) is a private, informal one-hour meeting with a Supreme Court judge or master and your spouse (and your lawyers if you have them).

It gives you and your spouse a chance to talk about your family law issues to see if you can agree about how to solve any of them before you go to court. And if you all decide that you need to go to court to sort things out, you can talk about the best way to move forward.

You don't need to take a lawyer with you to a JCC." [5]

Before you go to your JCC, you should have a very clear idea of what is a fair deal. Again, the word to really consider here is FAIR for both of you. That typically means fifty percent of assets of the marriage, equal parenting time, and support payments as per schedule. So really, when it comes down to its purest essence, a fair deal is exactly that—FAIR. There is no requirement for either party to agree to anything at the JCC.

Retainers

Once you have finally decided on your lawyer, you will be asked to provide a retainer. Typically, lawyers ask for $5,000. I am not really sure why this $5k is the magic number but it seems to come up a lot.

What I ended up doing is saying that I would prefer to start with $1,000 and see how we work together and take it from there.

This is actually very important, because if you happened to make a mistake and just retained a lemon, you will not be trying to get $4,000 back or more, after your first $1,000 runs out, and trust me, it will run out extremely fast! However, if you decide to keep your newly found lawyer and future pal for the next few weeks or months, hopefully not years, then it's very easy to refuel your retainer when needed. Most lawyers accept credit cards, so refilling retainers is very easy. One added benefit of paying through credit card is that you get rewards points. At least you get to collect something positive out of your high conflict divorce.

DivorceMate Calculations

I was told monthly support payments are calculated by a software program lawyers have access to called DivorceMate and are also referred to as Spousal Support Advisory Guidelines (SSAG). Specifically, I was led to understand that support payment computer calculations come from entering your income and your spouse's income—and Tada!—out come monthly payments for child and spousal support. Everything was supposed to be mathematical, so no need to worry. They emphasized that the amounts entered into https://www.mysupportcalculator.ca/calculate are very close to the numbers produced by DivorceMate...I entered the numbers numerous times and felt I had a pretty good idea where I stood.

However, throughout my journey I had over a dozen DMs (DivorceMates) produced, and they all had different support amounts! It did not stop there—the DMs from the other side had vastly different amounts as well! It turns out that there are a number of variables a lawyer can enter to alter the amount calculated by the program.

Just to name a few of the parameters that change the calculations are income, number of children, years of marriage, etc. If you are a commission salesman, business owner, or an individual who works overtime, then determining your income will be an argument, and different amounts will be inserted in the program. Your income may fluctuate from year to year, and the opposing side will do whatever it takes to calculate the highest possible income in order for you to pay the highest amount of support. If you have been working lots of overtime and/or receiving healthy commissions (extra income which is not guaranteed in the future), you may end up paying support calculated on your highest income. Determination of income is in itself an argument. There is also imputed income, which is the minimum income a spouse is considered to be able to earn.

Turns out in my case the opposing lawyer created a four-page DM. Even my own lawyer could not decipher how it was produced and what several line items meant. It produced abnormally high support payments, and I was told all I had to do was hand in my own calculations, speak to it at trial, and let the judge decide. All this time I had it in my head—not that anyone told me this—that judges had access to their own DM calculations and go by their own numbers. Turns out they rely one hundred percent on the submissions, and somehow for whatever reasons, the judge will pick one DM over the other to ascertain support payment amounts.

If the other side is producing cooked-up DMs, then it is imperative to work very closely with your lawyer to define a good strategy to speak to it when in court. If you or your lawyer must spend a long explaining to the judge why your calculations are correct, then that is what must be done.

As a side note, nobody was able to tell me how the DM software works in the background and how it calculates the amounts. Somehow this software has become the authority for support payment amounts in the court.

Separation Date

There are certain cases where defining the separation date is of huge significance. This is something none of the many lawyers I visited ever told me. In fact, I did not know anything about this until close to my trial date. All in all, the length of spousal support is largely defined by the length of your marriage, and now you can appreciate how important is to provide rock solid evidence that the separation date is what you claim it to be. It is not enough to say what the separation date is, unless it can be proven in court with rock solid evidence.

You would think this is an important piece of information your lawyer would tell you, right? Well not in my case, and I am sure not in the case of many.

There are some really important things you must do. I can tell you that this advice alone has the potential of saving you several thousand or tens of thousands in the future.

You must do the following:

- ✓ Send an e-mail to your spouse with a clear statement of intent to separate and/or divorce. Come up with your own words for this, but it has to be absolutely clear for any stranger in the future reading this e-mail that your intentions to separate and divorce are firm.
- ✓ Twice a month follow up with additional e-mails to your ex that you are taking concrete steps toward divorce.
- ✓ Stop making tax declarations together. Each of you must make a tax declaration individually (not as a married couple), and each must indicate on the tax forms that you are separated. Again, no lawyer ever told me this.
- ✓ Immediately separate your bank accounts. In the future you must demonstrate to the courts that you no longer have joint bank accounts. Since those changes will be date stamped, they will help you validate your separation date. I cannot over-emphasize this point—no matter what path of resolution you end up

taking, you must show unequivocally what your date of separation is. It is not enough to show just one piece of evidence, like one e-mail. You must show a true separation in multiple ways as discussed above.

- ✓ As part of your separation date, you must stop going out together and having meals together. Your entire lifestyle should be clear for the world to see you are separated. As for leaving the house, this is not very simple actually. In some cases, the one leaving the house loses certain rights and claims in the dispute.
- ✓ If you are on the high conflict path, then all your communications with your ex should be via e-mail and in English. Again, let me say that all communications must be done via e-mail and in English. You will need to show the judge these e-mails, and they must be able to read them. If they are not in English, then you need to pay for translation services later.
- ✓ Keep all your communications firm and to the point. Your ex may taunt you with inflammatory, defamatory lies, and all kinds of accusations. Do not let your emotions take over and type angry insulting messages back, lest they be used against you in court.

In my case, I ended up living in the suite of the house with a separate entrance, so it was somewhat tolerable. However, your situation may be different, particularly if you suspect any possibility that your ex will press false criminal charges against you. In that case you have no choice, and you must absolutely leave the house.

You also want to discuss with a lawyer, ahead of time, how exactly a peace bond works. You need to have a basic understanding in case you end up having to deal with false criminal charges.

Documentation

I am amazed how much paper lawyers have to deal with, and I personally believe all this paper is an insult to technology. We have available at our fingertips everything we need to produce, reproduce, organize, send, and share nearly all information digitally. Being asked to produce so much paper for litigation was difficult for me to accept, but it is the system we have. One of my lawyers used to get angry with me because he did not accept files in a Dropbox (cloud storage) and did not know how to use it. Yes, really.

When I had to respond to an application made by the other side, a different lawyer, asked me to produce a list of documents and print two sets. I did not know this at the time, but Charlie had absolutely no idea what he was talking about and did not know what he was doing. At that time, I had absolutely no need to print anything, but I did, because I did not know any better. I wasted a lot of time and money producing two huge binders of information which was never used. Before you go ahead and print anything, first ask if sharing that information in PDF is fine, particularly if you are in the phase of exchanging information with the other side.

Always try to share large documents through a cloud service such as Drobox, OneDrive, Google Drive, etc. This makes life much easier. Another benefit is that as you make any changes to the folder, it gets instantly updated for everyone.

I saw lawyers sending multiple e-mails with one or two attachments because the files were so big, they could not be sent in a single e-mail. Again, I have no idea why they do not simply agree on cloud sharing services. It really is the best civilized way to send and receive documents. Every time documents are requested of you, do your best to share them through a cloud service electronically. You may find that electronic versions are sufficient for many of the steps in litigation.

What is most important is making sure to produce and share those documents the best way you can in a timely fashion. Do not delay production of important documents, particularly financial documentation.

In my experience, it is paramount to have a good laptop and reasonable skills using it. You will need to develop a digital filing system that will allow you to keep track of every e-mail/letter sent and document produced. The convenience of having everything easily accessible in the cloud cannot be overstated.

I organized all documents by date and gave each name a title that would allow me to find the contents as easily as possible. I found that nearly all required documents before litigation can be shared electronically only. It is only when it comes to court filings for trial that I was required to print everything and submit various copies for the court registry, the other side, and for myself.

In the beginning I did not do a good job at keeping a good filing system, only later to spend a full couple of days organizing and filing all existing documents into an easy to find system.

I opted to create several folders:
- ✓ Court filings
- ✓ Correspondence with the other side
- ✓ A folder for each lawyer
- ✓ A folder for trial documents
- ✓ And several subfolders for each

All documents were named as follows:
    Date - description of document
For example:
    2020.09.23 – Joanne - documents - house – accounts

This way all documents get organized by date. I also recommend renaming each file to provide a description that will allow you to know what the contents are without having to open the document. If your case becomes really litigious you will be happy to know you have a record of everything.

Also make sure to create descriptive documents on a cloud folder, so you can access any important document from your phone as well. I cannot imagine going to court without having deposited all my documentation on the cloud. I was always able to send any available information to my lawyer any time.

Any updates to any document made would also be instantly available on all my devices—critical for anyone involved in litigation.

A friend of mine told me that when her ex changed lawyers midway in the process, he did so without any documentation and arrived empty-handed. This new lawyer had to request a copy of the entire file. I never heard if the file was transferred electronically, but if it was not, then I know how messy this file transfer could have become. It is in cases like this when you will be thankful to have every copy of each document neatly organized electronically.

Trust me...I never thought I would have to go back to court after trial and hated the idea of it, but I simply had no choice. Given the situation, I was extremely happy to have electronic copies of everything neatly filed away, because I had to transfer all of it to my new lawyer. It took me little time to move copies to the cloud and send them off, transferring hundreds of megabytes worth of files just like that, no paper involved. I can say with all certainty, that had I not taken the time to file absolutely everything, I would have been in serious trouble trying to get all those documents.

It is imperative you become extraordinarily disciplined in the art of electronic record keeping and filing. That means as soon as any document is produced, you immediately rename and file it in the appropriate folder. Do not wait for a pile of e-mails, letters, and documents to pile up before you file them. It can get messy fast, and it is very easy to miss and forget to archive documents if you wait until you have a bundle for filing. I got into the habit of filing and organizing frequently, and even then, it was easy to miss a document or two.

On occasions some e-mails are so wordy and long that it is easy to miss the attached pdf at the bottom of the e-mail. Keep an eye out for those attachments at the bottom of long-winded e-mails. Truth is, you have no idea what documents you are going to need in the future again, so keep them all neatly organized electronically.

PDFs

All exhibits in your Affidavit need to be numbered. To do so, these documents must first be converted to PDF and merged into a single large file with exhibits in the order you need to have them, with each page numbered. I highly recommend using the paid version of Adobe Acrobat for this stage of the process. You can rent it on a per month basis and will only need it for a month or two. The features of Adobe Acrobat will be enormously helpful if you are creating your own documents as a self-represented litigant.

Adobe becomes even more critical if you are preparing documents for Court of Appeal, as they require specific features in the final document.

Then there are the small documents with just a handful of pages with signature and stamps. Instead of keeping a hardcopy, it is better to get a PDF scanning application on your phone that allows you to take pictures of multiple pages at a time. It will create a single multi-page PDF document and save it on your phone. The advantage of having this application over taking regular pictures is that it saves the entire document as a single file in PDF, which is exactly what you need to archive. It is not advisable to store documents as image files, as they become difficult to deal with.

These applications are easy to find and download to your phone. Just search for "PDF scanner app for phone," and you will see a few options.

Not just for legal document archiving, but for most of your documentation in life, this application is great to help you properly file anything you want and throw away the paper. Always remember to back up your computer.

Views of the Child Report or Section 211

Adding insult to injury is quite common in the family law machine, and pouring salt in an open wound seems to be a favorite of the system. Two people who were taking care of children together for years now get to argue that equal parenting time is totally unfair. It seems the courts would like to assume one is an unfit parent and should not have equal time with kids… just because. So now you need to pay an expert to see why you were an equal parent before and why you should continue to be one moving forward.

If you have young children, you may need a Views of the Child report. It is a psychological assessment of children, and to some extent the parents, to determine what is the best parenting regime for children.

The difference between this report and a Section 211 report is simple. The Views of the Child Report takes only a couple visits to complete and costs under $5,000. A full Section 211 report can easily run into the $20,000 mark along with more than $5,000 in legal fees.

Bob, one of my lawyers, highly recommended I should have a Views of the Child Report done before going to summary trial, as it would be the most appropriate tool for the judge to determine the best parenting schedule for our children. I was also informed that a judge may disregard the report, as it is their prerogative to either accept or reject it as a piece of evidence to determine parenting time. In other words, it was clearly explained that this report is, at best, another roll of the dice, a very expensive roll of the dice.

The report was produced and basically concluded we were both good parents. Again, we had no history of abuse in our household, so there was nothing glaring that would indicate that fifty/fifty was not in the best interest of the children.

Looking back, I can clearly say the Views of the Child Report was a huge waste of time and money for my case. I was warned the report could be set aside in court. I was also told that since my kids were past a certain age, they could decide where they wanted to stay. However, I was not told I could go back to court in the future to ask for modification on parenting time if children requested different arrangements.

While I was advised by my lawyer that I should have a report done before the trial, I now know that it was on me to have been more diligent to ascertain the risk/cost/benefit formula of this process. Had I asked more questions, I should have been able to see this report was unnecessary. If I could go back and speak to Oscar in 2020, I would say forget the report.

It appears if there is no physical abuse and/or violence in your household, the safety of your children is not at risk, and they are over the age of twelve, I would say a Views of the Child Report may have little impact on your case's outcome.

I think it is worth repeating—a judge can also decide to either ignore or put little importance to the Views of the Child Report, so just because you decide to have one made, does not mean the judge will pay attention to it. However, there is another option, the full Section 211 Report. Perhaps it will carry more weight. In short, a full Section 211 Report is approximately $20,000 and takes a few months to schedule and a few more months to complete. It assesses three factors: needs of a child, views of a child, and the ability of a spouse to satisfy the needs of a child. Once done, a litigant may use it to apply for specific custody arrangements in court. As you can see, it is a long and expensive process.

Here was my dilemma: I was told to do this, and to get that, and get something else, because that is what I needed to make a case and go to trial. I had no idea about anything, so I followed my lawyer's suggestions, and did as told.

I now realize the truth is that every step of the way you have to somehow verify and validate every recommendation. Always be asking what the risk/cost benefit of the next actionable item is, and fully understand how the benefit outweighs the cost. In other words, understand how big a gamble each alternative really is and if it is worth taking.

I encourage you to ask, ask many questions, and find out all the options—particularly when those decisions cost $5,000 and three to five months extra time.

My problem was not in "what I didn't know," rather my failure to ask relevant questions to help us arrive at smart decisions. Anyone facing the possibility of losing the house, children, and eighty percent of one's salary can quickly turn into an idiot if not careful.

A friend of mine told me he had to become his lawyer's "slave" and do as he was told from the moment he retained him. If he started arguing or making things difficult for his lawyer, he was instructed his case would get dropped, that the lawyer would only continue handling his case as long as he remained obedient. My friend told me he accepted the conditions, and at the end he got most of what he wanted in court. So good for him, he "won" his case working under such an arrangement.

Counselling

Traditionally, counselling serves as an effective way to work through issues either before making the decision to divorce or to help maintain a healthy perspective during the divorce process. I met with four different counsellors and one psychologist, to see if they could provide me with some practical advice. For the most part, I found the sessions useless. However, I would not go as far to say you should not try it.

If your personality is one that you really chat with others and like talking about your experiences, then there is a good chance counselling is the right path for you.

I believe one of the reasons it did not work for me is that I am results-oriented. For example, if I ask what is 2+2 all I want to hear is 4. I didn't like spending too much time understanding how the 2+2 came to be…I need practical advice to get practical results. There are some of us who cannot spend too much time explaining how we feel about the number two, and then how we feel about the equal sign, etc.

I found that counsellors do not really give advice. Instead, they ask you how you feel about this and how you feel about that and what would you like see happen, etc. It's more about helping you blow some steam.

In case you are divorcing a narcissist, I highly recommend listening to Doctor Ramani on YouTube. She has produced some amazing pieces regarding this personality disorder and offers great advice on things to do and what not to do when confronted with this problem. Better yet, her advice is free.

False Criminal Charges

At first pass, we may think false criminal charges are uncommon, since we rarely hear about them in news coverage. However, according to the site "A Voice for Men," up to 70% of domestic violence allegations are considered false.

In an article titled "False Allegations in Family Court: Who is to blame?" a New Jersey judge was recorded as saying:

> "Your job is not to become concerned about the constitutional rights of the man that you're violating as you grant a restraining order, throw him out on the street, give him the clothes on his back and tell him, see ya around…we don't have to worry about the rights."
>
> This article goes on to say "False allegations of sexual abuse in divorce have become prevalent to the point, that a name has been given: the S.A.I.D. Syndrome – Sexual Allegations in Divorce. [6]

This problem is more prevalent than we are willing to admit.

For most of us, it is hard to comprehend what S.A.I.D. can look like if we have never heard of it, either in the news or from our inner circle. It is worth our while to briefly explore the story of a man who committed suicide because of it. I will not copy and paste the entirety of the following story, but some of the most relevant paragraphs highlight the extent of the problem:

> This article entitled "B.C. Man Pleads for Family Court Reform in Suicide Note," printed in the *National Post* reports, "In a scrawled and bloody suicide note found in the truck, he wrote: 'FAMILY LAW NEEDS REFORM. I recommend mandated lower costs and less reward for false claims of abuse. Parental Alienation is devastating. I loved my children as much as a husband and father could. I see no light. Recommend: an authority consistent during high conflict separations. It is exploited in family law.'"
>
> The article continued, "Two days before he died, Jeramey wrote his lawyer: 'I'm tired…Not only have I lost my children which by itself has torn me into, but I have lost all my assets in life …The level of cruelty brought on by what could have been a simple divorce was and still is mind blowing and I'm simply not the same person I was, and I expect I'll never see that person again.'" [7]

If you think false criminal charges are a possibility in your case, then moving out of the matrimonial home may be the only option you have, and likely sooner rather than later. This is the highest level of conflict, and serious legal advice is needed here.

It is worth our while to spend some time thinking about Jeramey's comment that his case could have been a simple divorce. I can understand how any person going through such antagonistic experiences could be changed forever. It only takes one spouse to want to inflict an enormous amount of pain to the other to bring hell on Earth. Unfortunately, if there is some money to be had, then the vengeful spouse will eventually find a lawyer equal to the task. The movie *Liar Liar* with Jim Carrey perfectly dramatizes how cases can escalate fast.

Parental Alienation

To some degree or another, there will be parental alienation in almost all divorces, particularly litigious divorces. In most cases very little can be done about it unless the parental alienation takes the shape of serious emotional, psychological, and/or physical abuse.

If your situation hovers at the lower end of the parental alienation scale, consisting mostly of your spouse trash talking you to your children, then speaking with a counsellor may offer tips on how to deal with it and how to communicate with your children. It is close to impossible to do anything about it through the courts.

If parental alienation has taken new dimensions where severe emotional psychological abuse takes place, then getting a Section 211 Report and going to court with it may be the only solution.

Children

Any reasonable individual will agree that children must be first, and no doubt this is the honest goal of mentally healthy parents. Having a broken marriage and getting drawn into a litigious divorce does not make any one spouse any less a loving parent. Nobody will argue that parenting is a challenge in the best of marriages. What quality parenting can be given when two spouses are embroiled in a high conflict litigious divorce?

If your divorce is amicable, then care for the children will fall into place as the two of you explore solutions. However, if your divorce is litigious, it is a different picture…typically before, during, and after a difficult divorce, spouses spend a large percentage of their energy on…well, litigating. Being fully represented takes some of the stress away, but only some. Sixty percent of your mind and emotions are engaged in litigation, twenty percent of your energy is used at work, chores, errands, etc. That leaves ten to twenty percent left of you to give to your kids—and that twenty percent is, shall we say, polluted or low quality. It is really hard to give your best twenty percent when the other eighty percent in your life is less than ideal.

In perspective, if you come down with a cold, feel terrible, have a temperature, runny red nose, messy hair, un-brushed teeth, but declare to have just washed your hands, would anyone be particularly excited to greet and shake hands with you? Sure, your hands are clean but the rest of you is not looking very good. Similarly, it is a real challenge to look your best for your kids when under duress. It is just plain hard hiding a cold.

Although all kinds of advice exists for parents after divorce, following are my best recommendations:
- ✓ Do not trash talk the other parent.
- ✓ Do not interrogate kids about the other parent's lifestyle.
- ✓ Do not use children as messengers.
- ✓ If you know you are simply not in the zone, consider skipping a play day or two, and use the time to clear the mind in your own terms.

The truth is you also need lots of **"me"** time during a litigious divorce.

I have read a number of blogs explaining the damage of screaming and arguing in front of the children when dropping them off at the other parent's house or talking on the phone. I have yet to understand this scenario—have they not heard of e-mail? In most cases, e-mail is absolutely perfect as it provides a chance to think things through and send when appropriate. Why would an ex be within twenty feet of the other or be on the phone knowing the likelihood of an explosion is at ninety-nine percent? If the children are old enough, why not leave them at the door of your ex's house when dropping them off, and make sure they get into the house while you keep an eye on them from the car? This type of safe distancing can prevent unnecessary negative interactions.

I've read divorcees' blogs describing how they have to "force" their children to be with the other parent and follow court rules or make sure they have a relationship with the other parent. Also, I am not sure how a parent can have quality time with the children if they are in a bad mood. If this happens, you may wish to let up for a week or two, regroup, rethink, try to find out why the kids do not want to visit, and work out new solutions. A counsellor may be able to offer new fresh ideas.

CHAPTER 6

Technicalities

There are some technical alternatives and situations in litigation that may or may not be relevant to your case but are worth mentioning.

Representation

There are three types of legal representation. This section touches lightly on each.

Full Representation

This is the best alternative if you can afford it, as the lawyer deals with all aspects of your case. It's always worth looking into the option of being represented pro-bono.

Self-Representation with Unbundled Legal Services

This is a type of service many litigants are unaware is available. Succinctly put, unbundled services means your lawyer will only do specific tasks as assigned to him by you.

Unbundled services are perfect if you are comfortable writing e-mails and drafting your own documents. After Bob fired himself, I decided the only way to go was self-representation, and I was definitely ready to do it. However, I would never have done it without Michael, my unbundled lawyer. Legal documents and going to chambers require highly technical skills, and to put it simply, you don't know what you don't know. Before completing any task, I would have it reviewed/modified by my lawyer.

This way I found a happy middle ground. I did all the work and got a great unbundled lawyer to review everything.

I had short-listed two unbundled lawyers, only one with litigation experience. I was able to know this because I asked both of them many questions. Needless to say, I picked the experienced one.

No Legal Representation

I have read stories of people who do this, so I believe it is possible.

Lawyer Quitting

As my case drug on, I started to put ever increasing pressure on my then lawyer, Bob. I grew anxious of having to wait weeks for actionable items to be completed and having to remind him of things that needed to get done. I started pushing more and more to the point that he fired himself.

I did not know it at the time, but lawyers can fire themselves, when they don't like the way things are going.

This point takes us back to the beginning of this book when we speak about meeting with a number of lawyers and retaining the one you feel will offer the best results. The working relationship with your legal representation has to be mutually professional, courteous, and respectful. If one party does not do their share of the work, then the case begins to fall apart. Taking an adversarial stance with your own counsel is a losing battle, and if it is going that way, it's better to walk away and find someone else.

Anecdotally, I spoke with a couple of friends who told me their lawyers would drop their cases if they did not follow instructions given. So once again, if you are going to pay big money to be represented and be told what to do, then you'd better do everything possible to work with a true professional you like working with. You will always be expected to pay your retainer on time, so it is only fair to expect your case to move forward in a timely manner.

Now in my case, I had been very proactive on all aspects of my case, so I had all the information nicely organized in my computer and e-mails. I had all the files. After Bob quit, I immediately retained Michael, my unbundled lawyer, and continued with self-representation without a glitch. No harm done, no problem. The foundation for my case had already been laid out.

Financing and Contingency

As a general rule, a lawyer working on a family law case on contingency is frowned upon by the courts and mostly discouraged. It likely requires permission from the court for a lawyer to enter into a contingency agreement with his client.

Financing is perfectly okay though. A lawyer can enter into a financing arrangement with their client any time, and the courts do not see anything wrong with such an arrangement. The lawyer only needs to know the equity in the family assets to understand if they should provide financing or not. I have already touched upon my personal experience with Charles and how he offered me financing after I fired him. His financing proposal actually confirmed I made the right decision in removing him from my case.

I will advise anyone to think hard and long before signing a financing arrangement of this nature. The risks can easily outweigh the benefits of entering into such a contract. Remember the story of Ms. Fotsch under the heading "Next Step, LawerUp!" She won her case and still lost everything under such an arrangement.

If, down the road, you don't like how the lawyer is handling your case, it may be difficult or perhaps impossible to fire them depending on the amount of money you owe. Perhaps you will be handcuffed owing an enormous amount of money you simply cannot pay and will have no choice but to stay with a lawyer you no longer like.

Also, by entering such a financing agreement, an aggressive lawyer now has greater freedom to be even more litigious. Potentially, it can incentivize them to draw out conflict for much longer. In the case of Ms. Fotsch, remember how it took nine years to go to trial? That's a hard one to understand!

A financing arrangement has the potential for spelling real trouble for the entire family, and I encourage you to think long and hard before entering into this type of arrangement.

Scheduling Chambers

This is one area that made my head spin, and to this date I don't quite understand how this is even possible. I kept pushing my lawyer to land a date for the summary trial ASAP. We were ready, we had all documents in place…it was just a matter of getting available dates from opposing counsel and matching to court availability. The date for a summary trial had to be booked two or three months in advance, so we needed ample time to book a two-day summary trial with advance notice.

When requesting available dates, the other side would only offer two days availability out of each month, making it impossible to match only those two dates with court availability. I kept pushing my lawyer to get at least six days availability from the other side in order to book a trial date, but the opposing lawyer kept saying they were really busy and had only two days out of each month. I knew these were just excuses to avoid going to court, as they had no motivation to make any changes to the already existing support payments.

I became increasingly anxious about waiting month after month to get dates and book a two-day summary trial. It got worse when my lawyer began to justify opposing counsel for not offering more availability dates. He kept telling me it was common to be unavailable during those particular months and there was nothing he could do to change that. At that time, I really began to question where Bob's allegiance was. The way I see it, if a lawyer takes a case it is because they are available to go to trial.

It was not until I self-represented that I was able to book chambers for our trial. I was more aggressive in pushing for availability.

This is one of those tricks you need to pay attention to. A lawyer can simply say they are not available to attend court until months later, and that is that. Apparently in that situation you need to make a separate court application and spend more money to get the other side to provide whatever it is you need to get. It does not seem to stop here. There seems to be all kinds of tricks to delay due process for a very long time.

Again, the big mistake I made was that we did not book a seven-day trial at the onset of my case. There was no real incentive for the other side to want to fix things, and they were successfully driving me slowly into bankruptcy. They did not succeed as I self-represented, but you can appreciate this can be a rather stressful situation.

From the Archives of Experience

The first lawyer I retained took nearly three months to send a simple one-page letter to the ex. The letter should have said something like this:

> "Oscar wants to proceed with a divorce and would like to do it in the most amicable way possible. Please contact me to discuss friendliest avenues of resolution suitable for both of you."

Instead, James, my lawyer at that time, took three months to write a long winded three-page letter. To make matters worse he made the letter "without prejudice," which means I could not later present it to the judge as evidence.

I was new to the entire process and did not know why it was taking so long to send a simple letter to the ex. I did not want to be rude, so I sent e-mails that were indirect. Instead of e-mailing something like: "What is happening? Why has the letter not been sent yet?" I wrote e-mails like: "It sure is getting difficult around here. I hope we can start soon." I was afraid to be impolite, so I was not addressing the issue in clear terms.

After the first week of not seeing any activity, I should have called James and demanded that letter to be sent. I should have changed lawyers after the third week of no results.

Though I will never know with full certainty why James failed with my case, I suspect he was not interested in working below the hourly rate he normally charged. He was a referral from one of those lawyer referral services and charged me a discounted fee. Because of this, I believe James never intended to really represent me and saw me as the client who would pay for his coffee.

I hope it is becoming crystal clear why you need to meet with four lawyers at the very beginning of your case and ask pertinent questions.

Once retained, your lawyer owes you prompt representation. That is, you should see actionable items completed in less than one week. Particularly, one-page, two-paragraph letters should never take more than a week to draft and send. It is reasonable to expect most correspondence with opposing counsel to be completed within forty-eight hours. Certainly, there is always some give and take during the entire process, but overall, you must always have a sense that indeed, your case is moving forward.

Remember, you are charged for every e-mail and phone call. Typically, you get charged on a per six-minute block, even if it is a one-minute conversation, so make sure you speak about a few items in one shot. Typically, I would write down all my questions on my phone/computer and compile a nice list of items that I could e-mail to my lawyer and then discuss on the phone. Always prepare for your next meeting/conversation, as you want to be as efficient as possible. Every minute with a lawyer counts, and wasting time is wasting your money. Time is money. This adage never seems to get old, particularly in litigation.

Once you have that sinking feeling your case is going south, then it is time to pull out. Now you will really appreciate the fact you are trying to recover $500 or $600 instead of $4,600 from your unused retainer. If you run into this situation, it is nice to know you are not waiting for a huge amount of money to come back to you. A law firm typically will return any remaining retainer promptly.

I spoke to a total of twelve lawyers and found that two of the lawyers I retained were already extremely busy and had no time for my file. My case was the cherry on top, or perhaps more like the cherry at the bottom of their in-box pile, and I felt like I was never moving to the top. They would take weeks and in some cases months to do something. If you see this happening to your file, it is time to consider pulling out.

Remember that list of questions I offered you to ask the lawyer at the beginning of this book? Now you know the reason I am advising you to ask as many questions as possible. If they are handling over thirty cases, you may end up doing a whole lot of waiting to check off your next "to-do" legal item.

Throughout the process you should constantly ask yourself:
- ✓ Is my lawyer genuinely interested in my case?
- ✓ Is my lawyer providing a clear road map for resolution?
- ✓ Is every decision being made jointly after a careful risk/cost/benefit analysis?
- ✓ Are actionable items being completed in a timely manner?

Making Mistakes

It is most appropriate to close this section with a thought by Seema M Dewan. These are truthful goals we can all strive for, no matter where we are. To not strive is the greatest loss.

What Leads You to Make a Mistake?

Fear

The lack of self-confidence leads to making a mistake. The thought, "I may not succeed in my task," must be removed. No matter how much you are struggling, if you continue to concentrate on positive thinking, you will find the way and the effort to succeed in your task.

Impatience

Wanting an outcome fast leads to making a mistake. It's important to have a goal and a time limit, but if the time is not reflecting the desired outcome, give yourself more time to do your very best. Don't entangle yourself so much in the time limit that you create a blunder that becomes hard to correct. Learn to be patient. Patience is understanding your willpower to complete any task.

Anger

Where there is fear and impatience, there is the seed sown of anger. Anger is the expression of one giving up on one's self. Anger itself is the biggest mistake. When one fills himself with the thought of anger, one destroys all the will power to remain positive. Anger is the face of negativity. It is disrespecting the power and strength within one's self to improve. It is the thought of denial that leads one to give up self-reliance. Hence the thought of anger must never be fed.

Envy

Anger leads to looking at others' success. It makes one want another's joy…another's success and another's life. When one invites the feelings of envy, one becomes handicapped. One becomes certain that his life is not full and perfect as another's. Such feelings create a void within. One loses the power to walk on his own path of inspiration. Such feelings must be recognized as not real. They are mere waves of desire in which one wants another's happiness. Happiness is earned by one's own merit. One has to learn to return to the dedication to earn his own happiness by his own effort.

Jealousy

Jealousy is the rage and fire where one wants no one to be happy. In this thought are spite and hatred. One loses the focus of being calm…being good. One is ruled with the thought of another's downfall. It does not matter anymore to that person how well he is doing. He just wants no one to succeed and be happy. Such a person drowns himself in innumerable mistakes. The best way to come out of this jealousy is to begin once journey once again by taking a road of gratitude rather than of intense desire. Thank all those that love you…help you…give you…and tolerate your shortcomings. Gratitude and reflection of how you need to serve others will slowly take out the poison of jealousy within you.

Greed

Greed is being insensitive to another's needs. When one wants himself to be satiated first, he makes many mistakes. The thought, "I must receive all of it," quickly makes one close to an animal. Greed is waking up each morning to one's own desires alone. What a pity that one cannot see another's needs. The determination that one must be fed first makes him fall many a times…in his own eyes, and of course in the eyes of those he thinks he loves.

What is a mistake?

A mistake is following a thought that is filled with fear. Since such a thought lacks self-respect, it holds no respect for anyone else. A mistake is done in the panic of haste and the desire for immediate self-satisfaction. It lacks self-reflection…it holds within a silent anger for not waiting and working till the time is right.

How do you recognize that a mistake is about to be made?

Before you make a mistake evaluate your state of mind thus:

- ✓ Are you feeling impulsive? If yes, give yourself time to think and don't act until the feeling to rush passes you by...
- ✓ Are you filled with the bitterness or anger? If yes, calm yourself down. Talk to yourself until the thoughts of being self-righteous pass. You are in the mode of being right when you are absolutely calm. If thoughts of being a victim are pursuing you, let them pass. You are strongest when you believe yourself to be above anyone else hurting and controlling you.
- ✓ Are you blaming someone else for your weak state of mind? If yes, stop and listen your thoughts. Can anyone force you to think weak thoughts? No...realize that circumstances weaken you and that you feel locked and caged in saying yes to the tormentor within you. You are believing that you are weak and miserable. Misery and fear leave you the moment you think with the wisdom of truth and goodness. You can be free of any cage if you are willing to turn yourself to a new start that is filled with courage and perseverance.
- ✓ Are you thinking that your life alone is filled with difficulty? Are you thinking that all others have much lesser to face? That's an absurd thought to follow. The greatest difficulty is the fear of facing the unknown. The common mistake is to believe that everything should be known to you. Rise above both. You are to face the unknown with known confidence. You are to overcome the mistake of being safe and facing no sudden changes. Be prepared. Be bold in understanding that in every moment you will climb with higher will power. Welcome the uncertainty. And welcome the challenges of the unknown. [8]

SECTION IV

Psychological and Spiritual Dimensions

CHAPTER 7

Personality Disorder

According to the American Psychiatric Association, [9] there are ten specific types of personality disorders, and while this book is not intended to explore them in detail, the article points out that disorders affect the following areas:
- ✓ Way of thinking about oneself and others
- ✓ Way of responding emotionally
- ✓ Way of relating to other people
- ✓ Way of controlling one's behaviour

In case you find yourself in a situation where you need to deal with a disordered spouse, you will do yourself a favour to have basic understanding of what is happening in your life. This understanding alone can help you achieve a greater sense of well-being and peace as you will be able to realize that only the person with such conditions is responsible for their actions, and all you can do is move on with your life. Keeping one's integrity is important in the life of any human, and keeping one's integrity during divorce is paramount, which can only be achieved by understanding one's condition and surroundings.

After reading court room stories and books on psychology, it seems the predominant reasons for a couple to end up in divorce court is because at least one spouse has a personality disorder. While it is completely natural to be upset and frustrated at turning a leaf in life in this way, it is not natural to refuse to let go of the way life used to be and attempt to impose one's will on someone else for the purpose of continuing a lifestyle that is no longer there. Unresolved, unhealthy emotions and the lack of desire to accept their risks, will likely result in high conflict. These individuals may not be able to fully appreciate the damage such strong attachments create.

Ending up in court is nothing short of a fierce battle, a family war. Unless some really dark events have transpired during the marriage, it is hard to understand why a couple would end up in court.

If you are dealing with a personality disordered spouse, the worst mistake you can make is to beg for a peaceful separation, saying things like: Please don't make us go to court, it will ruin us—please let's avoid this legal mess—can't you see how damaging this will be for the family—for the children's sake, don't do this. To a disordered spouse, statements like this will only add fuel to the fire and make your ex come back even more fiercely. If this is the case with your situation, chances are high your divorce will be resolved at trial.

Putting it into perspective, if John Doe goes to his doctor and says he thinks he is a tiger and wants to bite his boss at work, the doctor will refer John to the psychiatrist and make sure he begins medical treatment immediately. However, if the same John Doe goes into litigation because he wants financial blood and hurt his ex as much as possible, he does not get referred to a doctor. If he has the money, the system will be happy to oblige and help as much as possible. Going through this experience will stretch your mind to its outermost limits.

Very few people really have any grasp of what defines a personality disorder. It is not that people have never dealt with narcissistic traits, but rather most do not understand how to classify and categorize such traits—much less understand how they combine to make a personality type, nor know how to deal with it. The difficulty compounds when many counsellors and psychologists don't understand much about this condition either, much less how to give advice on how to deal with it.

To be fair, no psychological condition is a digital condition with a value of zero or one. Either you are completely clear from it or you have it one hundred percent. Mental conditions are more like a gradient that changes over time.

A perfect example is temporary depression. You may be feeling depressed over one particular thing that happened in your life—let's say someone just scammed you out of $2,000 and you feel depressed about it, but once you meet your friends at a party your depression disappears. It is just a passing phase, and all you need to do is shake it off, not much to it. In this case, your depression went up to say ninety percent when you got scammed and eventually moved down to zero percent when you arrived at the party. It is a temporary condition that changes over a short period of time. To suffer from depression on a continuous daily basis marks a more permanent condition that will be called clinical depression and requires more serious treatment and intervention.

The same goes with personality disorders. To be fair, we all, to some extent, display traits of this condition from time to time. Usually, people who want to go through life with the least amount of confrontation and healthy relationships with proper personal boundaries will be able to identify a bad personality trait and direct some personal efforts in correcting them. It takes time to improve, but it is the hallmark of a healthy personality to always strive for improvement.

I have read and heard about so many anecdotal personality disorder stories to understand that they tend to have seemingly unlimited energy to engage in conflict, particularly if they feel betrayed or abandoned. When a regular Jon Doe gets tired of conflict and believes enough is enough, he has a deeply rooted need to continue with a "normal life." This is not so for them. They will continue to engage in conflict until either one of the following three conditions happen:

- ✓ Hell freezes over.
- ✓ They realize they are indeed in pain and need to start some honest soul searching.
- ✓ One of you dies.

This may not sound very positive, but you will be doing yourself a great favor seeing reality for what it is and accepting it, the sooner the better. It is damaging to go through a divorce and everyday tell yourself, friends, and family, "I don't understand why they are doing this!" Making statements like this is a display of naiveté and lack of effort in understanding your own challenges, particularly in an age when you can get most answers on the internet.

A personality disordered individual may decide to use litigation as a form of control and keeping the "relationship" alive through a high conflict divorce. For them, a controlling, conflicting relationship may be better than none at all.

Things get more complicated when friends and family say things like "you have to make your spouse understand that they have to be reasonable" or "in the future they will see what a waste of money/time/life it was to litigate." Comments like this will make your head spin and you soon realize it is best to not answer these kind of off-the-cuff comments. It only makes you recognize this journey is yours and yours alone. The only people you can talk with who might understand are other survivors of divorce trials or divorce coaches.

I don't know all the intricate details, but in the case of Jeramey in the story mentioned earlier, and the false criminal charges he had to face, it is fair to assume the ex had severe personality disorder issues. The story of Jeramey is an extreme example of how far they are willing to go.

If you are divorcing a disordered individual, it is imperative to assess if false criminal charges are a possibility. If they are, you may want to make plans to move out very soon. You may want to keep your phone with you at all times and make sure to start recording the moment you feel a tense moment may start to escalate.

Below is a brief description of how a relationship of this type may look:

Neurotic Aggression
- ✓ The need of power and domination of others, with contempt for weakness.
- ✓ The need to exploit and manipulate others, viewing them as objects to be used.
- ✓ The needs for social recognition or prestige.
- ✓ The need for admiration of your ideal self.
- ✓ The need of personal achievement combined with resentment when others don't recognize you. [10]

In closing, most divorcees typically have a difficult time even in the friendliest of divorces, it is a torrent of emotions to deal with, and that alone is challenging enough. Divorcing a human with a personality disorder gives the word "divorce" an entirely new meaning in a different dimension. The biggest problem is the healthy spouse who remains naïve and ignorant about this problem, not making an effort to properly name it and identify it for what it is. It is this ignorance and lack of understanding which creates even more pain. Once the condition is given a name and behaviour understood, it will provide the awareness that you alone are responsible for keeping your own integrity, and self-respect.

CHAPTER 8

Fifty/Fifty Parenting

Most people will agree that fathers have an uphill battle to climb in family court. Perhaps for this reason some fathers do not put the necessary effort into litigation. They may feel they have little chance of getting a fair and equitable judgement.

No matter what your perception of the family justice system is, if you are a father, you must put a sincere effort into your case and strive for fifty/fifty. According to Liveabout.com,

"Children who grow up in fatherless homes have a greater risk of major challenges in life than those who grow up with a father at home." We might want to believe otherwise, and there are many children who have overcome the hardships associated with an absent father, but the truth is in the data.

The negative effects of a child without a father can be seen in countless studies and reports. The statistics show the importance of a father figure in the majority of children's lives.

According to "What Can the Federal Government Do to Decrease Crime and Revitalize Communities?" from the U.S. DepartmenCfor:

Suicide: 63% of youth suicides

Runaways: 90% of all homeless and runaway youths

Behavioral Disorders: 85% of all children that exhibit behavioral disorders

High School Dropouts: 71% of all high school dropouts

Juvenile Detention Rates: 70% of juveniles in state-operated institutions

Substance Abuse: 75% of adolescent patients in substance abuse centers

Aggression: 75% of rapists motivated by displaced anger [11]

Now you can appreciate that your fight for a fair fifty/fifty split shows it is not just about you. Not handling your divorce properly may result in a more rapid disintegration of, not just the nuclear family, but of society.

This section applies to healthy parents with healthy habits. It sure does not help if a dad has substance abuse, anger, or personality disorder issues or his house is a mess, making things difficult for a child to want to visit. The environment in a parent's house has to be such that kids want to visit. It would not be healthy if children have to be forced to visit either parent.

I cannot help but wonder if there is a hidden hand steering the results in family court to remove fathers from their kid's life. In an article titled "A commentary on the shared parenting myth" published in a *Voice for Men*, Family Life Educator Ruth Nichols penned a letter addressed to Family Law Attorney Santo Artusa who argues that shared parenting should not be considered. Ms. Nichols states "With all due respect, The Shared Parenting Myth is somewhat remiss. Shared Parenting is not the problem in divorce and separation; Shared Parenting is the Solution!" She goes on to say, "Shared Parenting means that BOTH parents are participating in their children's lives. BOTH parents are working TOGETHER, as a team, ensuring that their child is receiving the tools necessary to progress in life as a happy, emotionally healthy, physically healthy individual who can make age appropriate and progressive decisions. Sometimes that means two homes." [12]

It is clear, both, the experts and the studies arrive at the same conclusion: equal parenting is the best option for children of the marriage.

CHAPTER 9

Finding an Entirely New Meaning

At the beginning of this book, I mentioned, "Divorce is not just an ending—it is a journey of self-discovery, a great opportunity to grow, and yes, there is a light at the end of the tunnel as you are about to embark on a whole new life." Let's make good on this idea and understand that no matter how bad your case is, it will only be meaningful if you learn and grow from it. We grow in the face of challenge, and the greater the challenge, the deeper the understanding.

No matter where in the divorce conflict spectrum you find yourself, you will be undergoing loss. After all, it is the end of a marriage, and that in itself is a loss, no matter how friendly it may be. What to say of the highest conflict cases?

Likely you have gone through life thinking the purpose of life is having a good job, earning great money, finding partners to have lots of sex with, finally settling down with one human and having even more sex, having a house and children, going on vacations, etc. Tada! That is a successful life! Few other experiences will challenge your perception of the universe like a divorce, and a high conflict divorce truly has the potential to shift your right brain hemisphere to the left and the left to the right.

What if you find that the human you married and had children with wants to torture you through a 1,000 page legal-document complete with papercuts, rejoices in seeing you suffer, and will throw a party when you commit suicide? If a prospect like this does not make you re-evaluate the meaning of life, then likely nothing will.

It is time to turn to introspection and start asking the real questions about universal existence, which primarily are:

- ✓ What happens after death?
- ✓ What is true love?

Death is the graduation of life, and if you have not given it much thought yet, well, this may be a good place to start.

Buddha took a slightly different question: "What is the source of suffering?" Even though he was a rich prince, surrounded by exquisitely beautiful women, and had sex anytime he wanted, he left all that behind to find the answer to his question. He did not have to get divorced to be shaken to the bone and want to understand the deeper meaning of human existence. There are now 488 million Buddhists around the world, and one third of the world population is Christian. Very likely it means Buddha and Jesus did, in fact, find some very interesting information about the meaning of life... not to mention that other great masters have also walked the Earth and left their beautiful teachings behind.

What if, all along, your goal posts were actually wrong, and you have been putting all your energy and concentration to arrive at a place that is mostly a ~~marriage~~ mirage? Can this be possible? Nobody can answer this for you, as you need to do the homework to get your own answers, but this much I can say with certainty. To go through a transformative event such as divorce and not want to put in some soul-searching time is a wasted opportunity for growth.

> "Life is a challenge, meet it.
> Life is a game, play it.
> Life is a dream, realize it.
> Life is Love, enjoy it."
> [13]

Before we move to the next paragraphs, I should be clear this book is not about promoting a particular philosophy, rather about helping you start a new chapter in life with encouragement and healthy habits. Some of the following concepts may be a tad difficult to digest for some, so I propose this question: What is the reason we watch Sci-Fi movies if we already know none of it is true? Why do we pay $25 to see these movies if we don't believe them?

I personally loved watching *Guardians of the Galaxy*, just like countless others did, and I am pretty sure none of us believed any of it was true. It went on to make $869 million in the box office.

We don't need to know these movies are true, do we? The truth is these movies make us feel happy for two hours. That's it—the entire science about these movies is all about how they make us feel.

Before entering the realm of philosophy, do not get caught up in the intricacies or how debatable the words can be. The real question is, if your mind were to entertain such concepts would you feel better? Do you need to know the words to be absolutely true in order to feel good about life? It's much like watching a Sci-Fi movie.

Here's a verse taken from an eastern book titled *Bhaghavad Gita*, which I find quite moving. Some humans around the world have spent countless hours studying this volume with the aim of finding peace. It picks me up whenever I am in a dark place and I read it:

> The contacts of the senses with the sense objects give rise to the feelings of heat and cold, and pain and pleasure. They are transitory and impermanent. Therefore, one should learn to endure them.
>
> Because a calm person who is not afflicted by these sense objects and is steady in pain and pleasure becomes fit for salvation.
>
> The invisible Spirit is eternal, and the visible physical body, is transitory. The reality of these two is indeed certainly seen by the seers of truth.
>
> The Spirit by whom this entire universe is pervaded is indestructible. No one can destroy the imperishable Spirit.
>
> The physical bodies of the eternal, immutable, and incomprehensible Spirit are perishable. ...
>
> The Spirit is neither born nor does it die at any time. It does not come into being or cease to exist. It is unborn, eternal, permanent, and primeval. The Spirit is not destroyed when the body is destroyed....
>
> Weapons do not cut this Spirit, fire does not burn it, water does not make it wet, and the wind does not make it dry. The Spirit cannot be cut, burned, wetted, or dried.

It is eternal, all pervading, unchanging, immovable, and primeval.

The Spirit is said to be unexplainable, incomprehensible, and unchanging. Knowing the Spirit as such you should not grieve.

Even if you think that the physical body takes birth and dies perpetually, even then, O Arjuna, you should not grieve like this. Because death is certain for the one who is born, and birth is certain for the one who dies. Therefore, you should not lament over the inevitable.

All beings are unmanifest, or invisible to our physical eyes before birth and after death. They manifest between the birth and the death only. What is there to grieve about?

Some look upon this Spirit as a wonder, another describes it as wonderful, and others hear of it as a wonder. Even after hearing about, it very few people know what the Spirit is.

[14]

Dedicating some time to reading these lines has the power to help anyone undergo difficulty in a much better frame of mind, even if, in your world, none of it is true. After all, it is how the words make you feel, rather than becoming an investigative journalist to fact check every statement.

If everything in life is to have meaning, then your divorce may just make you doubt your past pre-conceptions and make you ask new questions. Hopefully, that is.

We all hear anecdotal stories of divorcees who were faced with such problems they took to the bottle and drugs, only to find themselves in much darker places later, not to mention those who commit suicide. Substance abuse can numb the senses and make one forget all troubles. But as the mind begins to fade with substance abuse, so does the vital forces in the body, and human life begins to escape…not exactly an ideal solution.

Pondering upon words such as that of Krishan above is infinitely safer than diving into the bottle or smoking ourselves into oblivion.

It does not matter if one rejects the passage above, the point is this: divorce may just be your launching pad into a spiritual quest.

Why not try the following suggestions:
- ✓ Hand over your grief, and hanker only for the Chief, then you will always be in bliss.
- ✓ While outwardly continuing your earthly battles in the broken land of the family justice system, it is well to consider surrendering to the greatest master.
- ✓ It is for you to ask many questions and to be open to receive the answers. If the questions are asked in earnest, then the answers will come from within and without. It is your journey, and you must become very good at walking it.

The following words, from a great teacher from the East, are sharp as a blade, with the power to penetrate deep into one's own mind and soul. They have the potential to help us fire new neurons and reshape our thinking about our daily routines:

> In the whole world each person, whoever he may be, will love another only for his own sake, not for the sake of the other. If he loves

and object, he loves it for the self alone, and not for the sake of that object. That self is the spirit, the true self, but, when the pure love of the spirit becomes tainted with body-consciousness, and the senses hold sway, attachment and selfishness arise. This inevitable leads to sorrow.

The body is impermanent. Death is certain for all. Even if someone were to live for a hundred years, he would still have to face death one day. Everyone knows that. But 'sn't it strange that the would-be dying are dying and feeling sorry for those who have already died? Everyone is sure to meet death and so everyone may be thought of as among the dying. Yet even though they themselves are dying, people feel sorrow and grief when thinking of someone who has died. It is as if death were a totally unusual and unexpected thing, rather than the natural conclusion that must come to all. This sorrow that comes on, particularly when someone near and dear has died, can only be there because of attachment. After knowing full well that death is certain, if you still worry about somebody, it must be due to the attachment which you have developed for that body. It is this attachment which is responsible for all your grief. Therefore, when someone has died the primary cause for sorrow is attachment, not love.

--Sai Baba

When someone near and dear dies, you feel a tremendous void. In the same way, you experience an emptiness after divorce. As we've discussed, whatever your spiritual inclination, I encourage you to fill the void with positive and encouraging thoughts, activities, and habits. Only then, can you begin to move forward in life.

CHAPTER 10

Otherworldly Justice

Any reasonable person will agree that it is very difficult to find justice here on planet Earth. It appears that the good old days of "innocent until proven guilty" are fading fast to give way to the new dawn of "guilty until proven innocent." However, are we ready to accept there is no justice in the universe? If we are ready to make this concession, then we are setting ourselves up for despair.

I am an avid reader of all kinds of philosophy, and I cannot find a more balanced view of the universe than the one that includes, amongst other concepts, the law of karma. This philosophy is the only way some of us can make sense of life and make it easier to be alive and more accepting.

It is only human nature to ask why—why this happened and why that happened to me— answers that are impossible to find in regular science like physics or chemistry. If we can for a moment entertain the real existence of the law of karma (much like we are ready to accept Sci-Fi movies for two hours), then we can at least believe divorce (and for that matter most events in our life) results from karma and is meant for us to learn from and grow. Then, just maybe then, we will be willing to accept there is a reason for these things to happen and hopefully accept them for what they are.

Jesus was clear on this: "those who use the sword will die by the sword." [15] What if we made somebody suffer before? Is it our turn to be on the receiving end? What if the purpose of this divorce is to live through it, learn, grow, and be happier? Jesus' statement carries the fundamental truth of karma. He just did not expand on it as he had other messages to deliver.

Obviously, this leads to the question, does the wicked spouse get a karma-free ticket for the evils committed in divorce? After all, the ex is simply carrying the karmic execution order for your suffering so they should not be blamed for it. According to Karma theory this is not the case, the executioner always has the option to do better, and making a mess is always attributed to the perpetrator. The evil spouse—and enabling lawyer—do accumulate their fair share of bad karma. Karma is the great equalizer of all humans.

Here's the reason I insist you only fight for what is fair, which is fifty/fifty of assets acquired during the marriage. This is the percentage split recognized by the law, and the people involved in your divorce will bear witness to your effort to achieve a fair and equal solution, as generally accepted by the Family Law Act. The last thing you want is to be the criminal spouse, and in the process, accumulate worse karma.

Karma theory is a tad too complex for most of us to grasp. Briefly speaking, we interpret it as saying, "Do good and good comes back to you, do bad and bad comes back to you." This is fair and close enough. Just to add a little coloring, the first definition of karma theory was put forward a few thousand years ago or so, and it was referred to as "Madhu Kanda" which means "Honey Part." Succinctly, it means that if you have 100 bees collecting pollen from 1,000 flowers and later the honey is collected, no one can ever tell which drop of honey came from which flower, it is impossible! Similarly, we cannot possibly know what happened in our past that is responsible for our present situation. All we know is we must become better humans with each experience, and we are not to create more bad karma only to end up in an endless cycle of bad karma creation and bad karma payments for eternity. Sounds a little grim, doesn't it.

It can really help our healing process to think of the idea of karma as being a universal law, complete, thorough, iron-fisted, and incorruptible, that no human has ever existed and will never exist who will be able to bypass judgement. This concept alone should give us all the reasons to make us want to become better every day.

This same law also applies to any revenge-filled spouse and enabling lawyer who perpetrate endless suffering and pain on their victims. This means it goes without saying that iron-fisted karma will judge them equally, and they shall be sentenced in the universe's high court. Think of the implications of this! It means we are fully, completely free and absolved from seeking revenge or even feeling depressed. We can completely do away with any thoughts of "eye for an eye, tooth for a tooth." We do not have to make anyone pay. There is already an infallible karmic system that will take care of it all. We only need to take care of ourselves.

Confusion may arise here with the question, "Then what is the purpose of this book?" If karma makes everything right, then why all the fuss about a fair and equitable divorce? The short answer is that we still have a civic duty to do the right thing. We owe it to ourselves and society to do our share finding a happy medium for all. One area of social balance is law and order. Without it, anarchy rules and life becomes miserable for all. Giving away the farm due to laziness, confusion, or as a disguised way of absolving one's sense of guilt does not help anyone. Monetary compensation can never make up for the inner and outer failures of any one spouse, everyone has to do their part in any enterprise.

What karma theory provides is peace of mind by helping us go through life as if in the eye of the hurricane. It provides a great incentive to grow.

CHAPTER 11

Remake Yourself

If you find yourself in one of those amazingly high conflict divorces where the prospect of losing your children and substantial assets is very real, then there is one path available to you—remake yourself by reshaping your thinking and by questioning your pre-marriage perception of life's purpose. The blow of losing a marriage, children, and assets has been enough to make many commit suicide or to destroy their lives on different dark paths. There is no minimizing the pain that such a blow delivers to any human under such stress.

At this juncture I would like to share some words of wisdom in regard to grief:

> Grief is the real preceptor, teaching caution, circumspection, discrimination, detachment, awareness, and vigilance.
>
> The heart of man has to be toughened, not hardened; it has to be made soft, not slithery; this can only be achieved by the blows of loss, grief, and distress. It is God's way of shaping us in the Divine mold. But

> man is blind to His mercy; he revolts at the
> first blow of the sculptor's hammer!
>
> *--Sai Baba*

One thing seems certain, and that is if one continues with previously held beliefs of human achievement, one is likely not coming out healthier and stronger from a divorce. The stronger you identify with property and relationships, the harder it will be to persevere after divorce. If, on the other hand, you begin to identify as a universal being where you, indeed, form part of a cosmic family, and the boundless universe is your home, then challenges on planet Earth will feel more like bumps on the road. This is part of the premise some great masters have taught us.

> Life is a bridge. Cross over it, but don't build a house on it, it is a river, cling not to its banks; it is a gymnasium, use it to develop the mind on the apparatus of circumstance; it is a journey, take it and walk on.
>
> *-- Gautama Buddha*

> We tend to move into the world's by-lanes, fascinated by the world of sense-enjoyments and worldly attachments and thus miss the true goal of life. [16]

This concept that you are indeed a child of the universe, eternal and infinite, has the potential to help you manage any adversity much better than not even considering it. What truly matters is your own perception of yourself and how you feel.

Admittedly, this section is grossly over-simplified. People spend a lifetime trying to remake themselves through arduous work, study, and various practices. The idea that a divorce may just be the seed you need to embark on an entirely new life journey is a valid point that needs to be made here, and one that you may wish to seriously consider.

Are we any less a human being if we take huge losses in our divorce? If we potentially lose the rights to see our children, are we any less valuable? Seeking a spiritual value has the potential to help us weather our losses with so much more dignity. In many cases it may just be the only path forward.

> If our present is but the result of our past, the habits formed are over a long period. But whatever be the nature of the character one has come by; it can certainly be modified by modifying the accustomed processes of thought and imagination. No one is incorrigible. By conscious effort, habits can be changed, and the character refined. By selfless service, by renunciation, by devotion, by prayer and by methodical reasoning and logic, old habits can be discarded and new one's acquired for taking us along the divine path.
>
> --Sai Baba

Diet

Diet does not necessarily pertain to food only; it touches on everything you consume into your system. Everything you watch and hear is also part of your diet as it is absorbed by your brain and will have a direct impact on your overall well-being. Divorce is already stressful enough, and nobody will want to recommend taking in additional sources of stress that do not help you.

I highly recommend you substantially reduce, or eliminate altogether, watching news on television or reading newspapers.

News is negative in nature, and ninety-nine percent of the time there is nothing you can do about it. All you can do is read bad news, get stressed, be sad or angry, and continue with the next piece of news. The body is already stressed enough during divorce, and it should not be overloaded with unnecessary sources of adrenaline.

This is the best time to read uplifting books with positive messages that will pick you up. Do your best to eliminate sources of stress such as gossip and news and replace them with soul food. It goes without saying that an exercise routine combined with healthy food habits will go a long way in helping your body maintain an overall healthy well-being.

THE NEXT RELATIONSHIP

Stories abound of marriages ending because one spouse found someone else, or one spouse got into a relationship before ending a divorce, or a spouse found someone else immediately after divorce. There are different schools of thought regarding relationships after divorce. Some insist that you should get into a relationship as soon as possible, others say one should wait one month for each year of marriage, etc.

Mostly a very critical element about divorce always seems to be missing: how did we get into this mess in the first place, and how do we avoid landing into the same quagmire again? After all, there are many stories of people getting married a second and third time only to have disastrous marriages again.

We really need to look at the reason of why we got into the first messy marriage in the first place, and the answer often times seems to be simple. Most of us humans grew up in dysfunctional families to one degree or another. We grew up watching our dysfunctional parents not having a good relationship and unconsciously began modelling. This modelling went deep into our unconscious minds and became a deep level programming of our minds and emotions, much like an operating system will make a computer work.

When looking for a partner, our unconscious mind began steering us as per its deep-rooted programming and we managed to find someone with whom we would likely have a dysfunctional relationship. We were not consciously aware of any of this happening. In fact, we were convinced we had just found the right human to marry and spend the rest of our lives with. In fact, likely we say to ourselves, "I will not make the same mistakes my parents made." Nobody explained to us how the unconscious mind works. Years later, BOOM! Divorce.

No matter how much time we take between relationships, the next one is likely to fail if we do not take the time to erase all previous negative programming and install a new, fresh, positive one—a type of programming that has a very firm grasp of what a loving, respectful, adult relationship with proper personal boundaries looks like. The following paragraph is taken from *Codependency for Dummies* by Darlene Lancer:

> Therapists and counselors see people with an array of symptoms, such as depression, anxiety, addiction, or intimacy and relationship issues. Clients are hurting and often believe the cause is something outside of themselves, like their partner, a troubled child, or a job. On closer examination, however, they (and many readers of the first edition of this book) start to see that, despite whatever else may be going on, their behavior and thinking patterns are adding to their problems – that is to say, their patterns are dysfunctional. Their patterns have an addictive, compulsive quality, meaning that they take on a life of their own, despite their destructive consequences. The root problem is usually codependency. [10]

True rewards can only come when we pay the true price, and we can only be rewarded with a good relationship after sincere soul searching and honest healing. Our standards need to be higher and understand that any relationship less than loving, respectful, and with proper personal boundaries is simply not worth having.

Some hints indicating you are in the wrong partnership include screaming, guilt tripping, lying, manipulation, gaslighting, constant contradictions, shaming, blaming, dismissiveness, regular invasion of personal boundaries, and playing victim. Hardly one of these traits happens on its own, usually they come in bundles. If you are living through this and "have gotten used to it," know that it is not healthy. Getting used to and living with it does not make it any healthier. If you are ending your marriage for any of the reasons above, it follows that your next relationship will be similar unless you do some soul work. The following paragraphs are taken from *Codependency for Dummies:*

> Denial doesn't always mean you are not bothered by their behavior. It means you do not recognize it for what it is, such as abuse, infidelity, an addiction, or other issue. The fleeting possibility may cross your mind, but you don't think about it. You may dismiss it as unimportant, or minimize, justify, or excuse it with explanations, and rationalizations.
>
> You're usually looking for someone to make you happy if you're single, and when you're in a relationship, you focus on making that someone happy. In neither case do you take the time to make yourself

happy. You're rarely content with yourself and become overly invested in pleasing or helping someone else, whom you begin to depend upon to fill in gaps in your Self. Soon you're reacting to and controlled by that person's feeling, needs, and behavior, and you try to control the other person to feel better, rather than honor your needs and feelings.

Many codependents have a chronic low-grade depression of which they are unaware. The excitement, romance, sex, an unavailable partner, melodramatic relationships, a busy schedule, and the tasks of being a caretaker provide sufficient stimulation and distraction from the depression that's just beneath the surface. A peaceful relationship or calm environment would soon be boring, without the Adrenalin that drama and stress create to mask underlying depression. [10]

CLOSING THOUGHTS— THE SMILING WARRIOR

In closing this book let me just say that
from the bottom of my heart,
<u>I truly wish you a peaceful and amicable resolution.</u>

May this beautiful thought encourage you:

The Smiling Warrior

In the middle of the toughest battle you have to say to yourself, "I must continue the battle and not let the enemy of fear within me win."

It's normal to be overcome with hopelessness once in a while. But you have to talk yourself out of it. Your dreams and goals must not die because of a pebble...a rock...or a mountain before you. You are capable of climbing over all the three.

In trying to see a glimpse of what may happen and what may not happen, we often lose the time to see what is happening right now. Don't plan your battles. Fight them moment to moment.

We are often too concerned on how much effort we need to put in. We want to know and measure the worth of our effort versus time. That creates the difficulty we fear so much. To do your best you have to be it. Being your best will give you immense peace. The difficulty vanishes where the best self survives.

We are afraid to smile and fight our battles. We want to smile only after we receive the results we desire. Imagine years of living in fear and hopelessness and only living a moment of a smile. Let's turn that around. Let's smile in the toughest circumstances. Let's reach the results when it's time. And let's accept the results to be the stepping-stone to the next direction. It will all fall in place. Be steady in your strength to face the moment you are in right now.

We often feel that we have the most difficult lives. The moment you become resistant to what you receive you create a difficulty. The difficulty is your denial of you facing the present. One battle ends and the other one begins. That's the essence of life. We have to enjoy the battle…the small defeats…the victory and the new chapter to come. We have to be the smiling warriors that overcome the taunts and doubts of the inner enemies in us. [17]

ABOUT THE AUTHOR

Oscar Chavarria's introduction into the world of litigious divorce fueled him to be a light in the darkness for others. Determined to guide people through the good, the bad, and the ugly parts of divorce, he penned a book full of helpful advice in hopes of stopping even one person from making the same mistakes he did. Divorce is a journey fraught with dangers, pitfalls, and blind spots, so he knows there's no such thing as being overprepared.

Oscar has an extensive career background as an electronics technician and salesman and has traveled across North and South America. His journeys have introduced him to all kinds of people in all walks of life. He's an avid reader with a particular love of Eastern philosophy and psychology. While searching for the meaning of life, he travelled to India multiple times and still seeks to understand the world around him—and the people within it—better. He hopes that knowledge will equip him with the tools to make the world a better place for others. The Good, The Bad, and The Divorce is his debut book.

For additional information about the author visit
www.lifebridgecoach.ca

BIBLIOGRAPHY

[1] K. Tomlinson, "B.C. woman may lose home over huge lawyer bill | CBC News," 4 December 2012. [Online]. Available: https://www.cbc.ca/news/canada/british-columbia/b-c-woman-may-lose-home-over-huge-lawyer-bill-1.1291889.

[2] S. Tzu, "The Art of War," [Online]. Available: http://classics.mit.edu/Tzu/artwar.html.

[3] S. M. Dewan, "Inspiritional Writings by Seema M Dewan," 1 January 2022. [Online]. Available: https://www.facebook.com/SeemaMDewan.

[4] S. M. Dewan, "Inspirational Writings by Seema M. Dewan," 19 Janauary 2022. [Online]. Available: https://www.facebook.com/SeemaMDewan.

[5] LegalAid, "Judicial Case Conferences in Supreme Court," [Online]. Available: https://family.legalaid.bc.ca/bc-legal-system/if-you-have-go-court/jcc-supreme-court.

[6] R. A. Nichols, "False allegations in Family Court: Who is to blame?," 19 April 2016. [Online]. Available: https://avoiceformen.com/featured/false-allegations-in-family-court-who-is-to-blame/.

[7] C. Blatchford, "B.C. man pleads for family court reform in suicide note," 9 May 2017. [Online]. Available: https://nationalpost.com/opinion/christie-blatchford-b-c-man-blamed-cruelty-of-family-court-battle-for-driving-him-to-suicide.

[8] S. M. Dewan, "Inspirational Writings by Seema M. Dewan," 19 December 2021. [Online]. Available: https://www.facebook.com/SeemaMDewan.

[9] American Psychiatric Association, "What are Personality Disorders?," American Psychiatric Association, November 2018. [Online].Available:https://www.psychiatry.org/patients-families/personality-disorders/what-are-personality-disorders.

[10] D. Lancer, Codependency for Dummies, Hoboken: John Wiley & Sons, Inc., 2015.

[11] W. Parker, "The Troubling Statistics on Fatherless Children in America," 24 May 2019. [Online]. Available: https://www.liveabout.com/fatherless-children-in-america-statistics-1270392.

[12] R. Nichols, "A Voice for Men," 27 February 2016. [Online]. Available:https://avoiceformen.com/featured/a-commentary-on-the-shared-parenting-myth/.

[13] S. Baba, "A quote by Sathya Sai Baba," [Online]. Available: https://www.goodreads.com/quotes/191399-life-is-a-game-play-it-life-is-a-challenge-meet-it.

[14] K. "American/International Gita Society Bhagavad Gita," [Online]. Available: https://www.sacred-texts.com/hin/gita/agsgita.htm.

[15] J. "Matthew 26:52," [Online]. Available: https://biblehub.com/matthew/26-52.htm.

[16] S. Vivekanda, "Feature Articles: The Vision of Non-Duality - April 2006," [Online]. Available: https://archive.sssmediacentre.org/journals/Vol_04/01APR06/equanimity-nonduality.htm.

[17] S. M. Dewan, "Facebook," 13 February 2021. [Online]. Available: https://www.facebook.com/SeemaMDewan/.

www.ingramcontent.com/pod-product-compliance
Lightning Source LLC
Chambersburg PA
CBHW050246120526
44590CB00016B/2236